The Marketing Mirage

The Marketing Mirage

How to make it a reality

Colin McIver

NICHOLS PUBLISHING COMPANY : NEW YORK

First published in the United States of America in 1987 by
Nichols Publishing Company,
Post Office Box 96
New York, N.Y. 10024

Library of Congress Cataloguing-in-Publication Data

McIver, Colin, 1914–
    The marketing mirage.
    1. Marketing   I. Title
    HF5415.M2583 1987   658.8   87–14048
    ISBN 0–89397–285–1

Printed in Great Britain

Contents

To my long-suffering clients, particularly those who sometimes took my advice

Preface

I have been very lucky in the opportunities my working life has given me over the last forty years to learn about the practice of marketing. Working for all sizes and shapes of organization – first as a market researcher, then as an advertising agent, and finally as a marketing consultant – has involved me as both participant and observer (from several different viewpoints) in the development of practical marketing thinking.

In some ways it has been a disillusioning experience. Certainly the high hopes of the early post-war years that marketing would be the answer to all economic problems were soon disappointed; once post-war shortages had put an end to the sellers' market, it became sadly clear that a multitude of marketing managers had not greatly improved the ability of producers to satisfy their customers. Nor has the refinement of research and advertising techniques or the elaboration of marketing theory in business schools and other seats of learning greatly influenced the realities of commercial life. Companies all willingly concede that the customer is king (or queen), yet still treat him (or her) with the utmost lack of consideration. Indeed there is a growing and disturbing gap between marketing theory and commercial practice.

The main thesis of this book is that marketing, if it is to become a real force in business, politics and other fields of human endeavour, needs to infect the bloodstream of organizations; and that marketing men and women need to think more about indoctrinating their colleagues in whatever situation they find themselves than about forming an exclusive club which knows all the marketing rules. The rules are all very well; but they won't work unless they are adapted to fit the circumstances and the people involved. This is as true in the United States and other western countries as it is in Britain, the source of most of the examples in the book.

Henceforward I shall abandon laborious use of phrases like 'him or her'. To save unnecessary verbiage I shall generally confine myself to the masculine noun or pronoun, using it in a strictly sexless sense.

Part One

Marketing is Management

The first part of the book explores the reasons why marketing – the white hope of the early post-war years, and still coupled with motherhood and efficiency as unquestionably desirable – has failed to deliver the goods. Business schools teach it; managements, no matter how introverted, preach it; but the anticipated revolution in the behaviour and success rate of organizations, whether governmental or commercial, has not taken place.

A tentative conclusion is that marketing specialists have overplayed their hand, claiming a magico-therapeutic effect for marketing techniques which could only be achieved in conjunction with effective general management in a favourable corporate climate. The fact that marketing became fashionable in the 1950s, when the previous ten years of deprivation made it easy to sell anything, led to the false conclusion that marketing could work in isolation. It would have been wiser to promote marketing as an important element in a co-ordinated management mix than as a wonder-working additive.

This more modest approach is adopted in suggesting ways in which the general manager and the marketing specialist can work more constructively together – and in the end (who knows?) become one and the same.

1 The revolution that didn't happen

Remember the 1950s? Well, come to think of it, you probably don't. So let me tell you what it was like to be a marketing man in those early, hopeful post-war years.

It really looked like the dawn of a bright new day. We had won the war (we thought). We had dreams of a newer, more just society in which the benefits of ever-increasing prosperity, fuelled by the new technology which the pressures of war had encouraged, would be shared so that everybody who sincerely wanted to be rich could be rich and nobody need be poor. And scientific marketing, the skill that we claimed to have mastered, was going to be the catalyst that would make it all come true. Marketing would revolutionize management and galvanize dull old sales and boring old production; the backward-looking accountants had had their day and would give way to the forward-looking marketers.

Everybody was ready to be led by marketing into a brave new world. The techniques were there, albeit borrowed from the Americans. The climate was right; when people were starved for consumer goods, it wasn't too hard to persuade yourself and others that you were brilliant at marketing them. The marketing revolution had arrived and you were marching in the van. As Wordsworth remarked of an earlier, less bloodless revolution:

Bliss was it in that dawn to be alive
But to be young was very heaven!

It doesn't seem to have happened. While Britain has certainly made great gains in material prosperity over the last thirty years, we have steadily lost ground in comparison with other developed countries. From being one of Europe's richest nations, we have drifted into being one of the poorest. Despite all our pretensions to marketing expertise (in the 1950s we regarded ourselves, not without justification, as well ahead of the rest of Europe in this respect), we have steadily lost our share of world trade and finally achieved the remarkable record, for the forerunner of industrialization, of an unfavourable balance of payments in manufactured goods. Even the marketing-oriented American Economy has its balance of payments problem. Though the inventors of the welfare state, we can no longer afford, we are told, to keep up with our now more affluent neighbours in the provision of social benefits and the preservation of social amenities. There is scant evidence of the marketing battle-cry (we thought it a cliché) that the customer is king being widely recognized and put into practice. And the accountant still rules the roost, pursuing solvency if not prosperity through cost-cutting, rationalization, mergers and redundancy.

What went wrong? More importantly, what can be done in the marketing context to enable the marketing philosophy and its practitioners to make a more effective contribution to the health, wealth and happiness of this nation and of others? The climate is certainly not as favourable as it was thirty years ago. There is considerable scepticism about the practical value of marketing, even though its philosophy (if it can be dignified by such a word) and its techniques are not seriously questioned. Perhaps by considering with due humility the reasons for its frequent failure to achieve demonstrable success, it will be possible to construct a realistic rulebook for marketing in a cold climate which will improve the success rate of marketing in general and its individual practitioners in particular.

But from now on it *will* be a cold climate. It will be cold in the sense that customers and intermediaries are now much more sceptical of marketing propositions, much more conscious in a highly competitive environment of their power to play off one supplier against another. It will be cold also in the sense that any disposition on the part of managements to regard the marketing man as a knight in shining armour, who can be counted on to save a desperate situation, has long since vanished; he is just another competitor in the managerial race, another threat to established positions, particularly uncomfortable in his insistence on advocating change.

Marketing as *deus* (or *dea*) *ex machina*

It all sounded so easy, if you read the right textbooks. There was poor old company X, grievously production dominated, churning out obsolescent products on obsolescent plant, bullying a harassed sales manager into selling the stuff somehow or other to somebody or other. Along comes the marketing hero or heroine, preaching the gospel of customer orientation.

An applauding audience rallies round, while he or she (actually it seldom seemed to be she, though equal opportunity is progressing) advances majestically down the prescribed road of market research to identify customer needs, product development to meet those needs, product testing to make sure you got it right, the marketing plan, test market and fully orchestrated launch – to the guaranteed pot of gold.

But somehow that's not the way it turns out. Far from applauding, the audience does its best to trip up the new broom. The smooth progression down the textbook marketing road falls victim to Murphy's law, and everything that can go wrong does go wrong. And more often than not the promised pot at the end of the road contains not gold but the depressing message 'Write it off and get back to the drawing board.'

There have been successes

In seeking to learn from the past, it is as misleading to be too gloomy as to put too bright a face on it. Many new markets have been built over the past thirty years and many companies or products have prospered in these new markets, as well as in long-established markets. A marketing historian could look at the fast moving consumer goods field and commend the alternating triumphs of the Procter & Gamble and Unilever marketing men in creating a market for oil-based detergents and for such brands as Tide, Daz, Omo and the rest. Or he could look at the field of distribution and describe the development of self-service and supermarkets (which for better or for worse have revolutionized the nation's shopping habits), commending the marketing success of multiples like Sainsbury and Tesco or A + P in creating distinct identities for themselves. Or, turning to the industrial sector, he could talk of the meteoric, all-pervasive rise of the computer and of the marketing imagination shown first by IBM in analysing the needs of different user industries and selling a tailor-made service rather than a lump of expensive hardware.

But were these purely marketing successes? The answer is clearly no. In each case success was dependent on a concatenation of favourable circumstances, and only a partisan historian could claim the lion's share of the credit for marketing. Synthetic detergents got their start from a combination of technological development (they were more efficient than soap for use in washing machines, particularly in hard water areas), a favourable economic climate (soap was rationed when they were introduced and increasing prosperity in the post-war years encouraged change) and, particularly important for the marketer, company organizations and attitudes which encouraged marketing innovation.

The self-service and supermarket revolution was not stimulated by the kind of consumer demand that marketing theory seeks; the benefit of pushing a trolley down the supermarket aisles and queuing at the check-out, compared with being waited on by your friendly neighbourhood grocer, was not immediately obvious. But such circumstances as the rising cost of labour, the increasing variety of packaged goods to be stocked and the economies of bulk purchase made it expedient for retailers to move towards larger, more automated premises – and to persuade the customer to do more of the work; while relatively lower prices, wider choice and more private cars to ferry the stuff home made a change of shopping habits acceptable. Marketing certainly played its part; but it was not a solo performance.

Nor could the computer revolution be regarded as led by marketing. If anything it was technology, making it possible to store much greater quantities of information and process it much more rapidly, that led the way, and the increasing size and complexity of commercial and industrial organizations that gave technology its outlet. Marketing had simply (not all that simple, actually, or all that well done) to build the bridges between the computer technologist and the clearing banker, the mass distributor or the mass producer whose business could not achieve its growth targets without the aid of the well-tempered computer.

I have no wish to depreciate the contribution that well-planned and efficiently executed marketing can make to the success of any organization; or to deny the need for most organizations to be more interested in the customer and less in their internal affairs than they are today. But marketers and those who look to marketing for a solution to fundamental corporate problems should not be unrealistic in their expectations. Marketing successes (or failures) are seldom attributable to marketing alone. It is a combination of factors – a favourable external climate, a competitive advantage in technology or operational efficiency, effective management controls *plus* the marketing ingredient – that makes the difference between success and failure.

To illustrate this holistic argument, let us consider Hans Andersen's sad story of the Emperor who had no clothes.

The Emperor who had no clothes: A tale of our times

Then the Emperor walked along in the procession under the gorgeous canopy and everybody in the streets and at the window exclaimed, 'How beautiful the Emperor's new clothes are! What a splendid train! And they fit to perfection!' Nobody would let it appear that he could see nothing, for then he would not be fit for his post, or else he was a fool.

None of the Emperor's clothes had been so successful before.

'But he has got nothing on', said a little child.

The following, in all its essentials, is a true story; only names and details have been disguised to protect the gullible and the guilty.

The executives of the South Riding Development Authority were as enchanted as Hans Andersen's courtiers when Julius Keyser came to them with his proposal to reactivate the recently closed Three Rivers seed crushing mill. Its closure, with the loss of 100 jobs, had been a considerable disaster in an area where unemployment was already painfully high; and there was some feeling that with a livelier, better informed management the disaster might have been averted.

Julius Keyser was nothing if not lively. The professionalism of his presentation contrasted impressively with the amateurism of the inventors and other aspirant entrepreneurs by whom the authority was usually confronted; you could almost have believed that he had practised on other development authorities in the past.

He had at his fingertips a dazzling assortment of facts and figures about the seed crushing industry worldwide, with some interesting suggestions about new raw material sources. His profit forecasts appeared to be well documented. And best of all he was prepared to put up £100 000 of his own money to supplement the £500 000 in investment capital, loans and grants he sought from the development authority.

The authority was convinced. In fact it fell over itself with enthusiasm. For the project promised to kill two quite different birds with one stone. Not only would it help in a small way with the employment problem which it was the authority's main purpose to ameliorate, but it would provide belated justification for an earlier miscalculation, when the authority had invested in a large granary to store imported grain for the local millers and feed merchants. They had not foreseen the changes in farming practices brought about by the Common Agricultural Policy grant system, as a result of which the South Riding became self-sufficient in grain – leaving the authority with a handsome empty granary. A million tonnes of imported soya beans would come in very handy.

The authority's bankers, the Bogshire Bank PLC, were more sceptical when approached by Mr Keyser for loan capital, despite the authority's warm recommendations. They had seen other apparently promising ventures fall flat before. But this little difficulty was overcome when the authority indicated to the Mudshire Bank that they could expect to get the prestigious (and government guaranteed) development authority account away from their arch-rivals the Bogshire Bank, if they could see their way to obliging in this instance. They were indeed happy to oblige and agreed to put up a further £500 000 of loan capital, taking a charge on the plant and equipment.

At this stage Julius felt pretty pleased with himself. He had £1 100 000 in the kitty – enough to buy the plant and equipment from the receiver at the knock-down price he had negotiated and leave a substantial amount over for start-up costs and working capital. And he had arranged the capitalization of the business so that his £100 000 outranked the minority shareholding the development authority had insisted on. (In the event it turned out that it was not actually his £100 000 but was made up of speculative investments by some rich friends and associates in his home country.) He felt pleased enough indeed to appoint himself chief executive at an annual salary of £50 000 tax free (payable in an offshore tax haven), to recruit key members of the old management and workforce to use his undoubtedly extensive knowledge of the seed crushing industry to get back into business.

His method of doing so was somewhat curious but understandable in a situation where cash was still tight. He ordered supplies of soya bean not perhaps at the best available price, but from a supplier who was prepared both to offer 180 days credit and to dispose of the meal that was left after the seed was crushed. He also arranged to sell the unrefined oil that emerged from the crusher, again not perhaps at the best available price, but to refineries that were prepared to pay cash.

The result was a positive cash flow over the first six months, before the suppliers' bills were due, which proved most heartening to the bank – though in fact the company was consistently trading at a loss. As a token of its increased confidence, the bank agreed to an overdraft of £500 000 to cover working capital requirements. On the strength of this Julius too felt confident enough to set up a property company subsidiary, which in its turn invested in a stately home for the use of the chief executive on his visits to the South Riding – not all that stately, but stately enough to necessitate the acquisition of a chauffeur-driven Jaguar to keep up with the neighbours.

At this point it would be as well to pause and reflect upon the nature of the seed crushing industry – something which the development authority and the bank might usefully have done before entrusting themselves to the prestidigitatious hands of Julius Keyser. Seed crushing, as a couple of weeks' serious investigation could have told them, is a relatively small low-margin business, sandwiched between the much larger businesses of oil seed growing, trading and transporting on the one side, and the production and marketing of products using vegetable oils as an ingredient and the marketing of meal for animal feed on the other.

On the production side, world prices (it is a world commodity market) are highly volatile, depending on more or less uncontrollable factors like weather and politics. But the range of fluctuation for any one seed is controlled to some extent by the fact that one can often be substituted for another in blended end products. For example, six years ago the ratio of soya bean oil to rape seed oil in

UK produced margarine was approximately 75:25; now it is nearer 55:45, owing to the increased (some might say excessive) production of rape by EEC farmers. Latterly an energetic marketing drive by the Malaysian government to increase exports of palm oil has further confused the situation. This is in no way upsetting to the end product producers, who can play one supplier off against another; but it is no help to the seed crusher, whose plant and supply channels may be adapted to only one type of seed.

The business of processing and marketing end products based on vegetable oils downstream of the seed crusher is equally volatile. Here demand and price fluctuations are related to consumer taste and the price or availability of alternative products. Using margarine again as an example, consumption and price levels are affected by such factors as consumer purchasing power, the prevailing price of butter and health propaganda.

The problem for the seed crusher is that while raw material prices and end product prices are related in the long run, in the short run they are independent variables – and if the wide fluctuations on either side both go against him his small margin in the middle can be crushed to extinction. Moreover even the good times do not last long for any but the most efficient seed crushers – who tend, because of the economies of scale, to be the largest.

The consequence of these hard facts is that seed crushing has progressively been concentrated in the hands of large vertically integrated organizations like Unilever, Continental Grain and Tradax, which can gather all the benefits of size, as well as captive raw material sources and end product outlets; and when times are hard, can absorb seed crushing losses in the overall profitability of their operations.

If challenged by investors and bankers to explain how in the circumstances his business could survive over the long haul, as regrettably he was not, Mr Keyser would no doubt have held forth about the advantages of the site he had found for the mill (most existing mills were in the west of the country, whereas he could claim to supply the east coast population, which was more than large enough to absorb the quantities of oil and animal feed he had in mind). He could also have made much of the flexibility of a small operator, run by a nimble entrepreneur, who could take advantage of spot buying opportunities for raw materials and exploit local shortages to get a good price for his end product.

The trouble with the first argument, when closely examined, was that the isolated site was a disadvantage rather than an advantage; the local port could not accommodate bulk carriers of imported raw materials, thus increasing costs, and the local population whether human or animal could not consume the oil or feed meal until they had been respectively refined or compounded. The refiners and animal feed compounders were needless to say all closer to the large mills in the west than to the east coast site of Keyser Enterprises – resulting in a significant delivery cost penalty.

But the backers and the bankers were now too heavily committed to the project to ask awkward questions at this stage. What they were looking for was evidence to allay their misgivings about the unprofitable trading results so far (after all, you expect an unprofitable period when you are starting a new enterprise) and to support their hopes that everything would come good in the end. They introduced financial consultants who prepared new cash flow and profit forecasts in meticulous detail. They were all based in the end on Mr Keyser's exceedingly optimistic forecasts of gross margins. But their very bulk and detail was reassuring. Even the gross margin forecasts could be justified up to a point by reference to a brief period in the past when raw material prices had been unusually low and end product prices exceptionally high, putting even the least efficient of seed crushers temporarily in clover.

To leave no stone unturned, Julius Keyser himself, acting on behalf of Keyser Enterprises, commissioned a firm of marketing consultants to undertake an independent study of trends in the seed crushing industry. They did an entirely competent job within the confines of the brief they were given. They confirmed that total UK consumption of edible oils was likely to be as high as Mr Keyser claimed, and that the mill's total output would represent a very modest market share. They confirmed that the oil and meal produced by the mill were of sufficiently high quality to satisfy potential customers. They confirmed that world availability of raw materials was likely to be more than sufficient, barring major crop failures, to satisfy demand. They confirmed that the firm's marketing methods and organization were as efficient as could be expected, given the small size of the organization. What their report – or at least the edited version of it given to the backers by Mr

Keyser – failed to say was that a very large part of the theoretically available market was not in fact open to an independent company because of the domestic trading arrangements of the large vertically integrated groups. Any internal efficiency the company could boast was far outweighed by the extra transportation costs resulting from its unfavourable location and by the higher raw material costs and lower selling prices it must expect in competing with its giant rivals in what was essentially a commodity market. It failed in fact to remark, because the brief did not invite it to do so, that in this market a small company lacking a highly specialized product had an outside chance of occasionally making a small profit and a virtual certainty of usually making a thumping loss.

In the event the losses did build up over the next six months to a level where cash shortage was once again a problem, the bank was making uneasy noises about the overdraft limit being exceeded, and something needed to be done to raise the wind if the company was to continue trading. Julius Keyser's assurances to the backers that trading conditions were unusually difficult – the state of the economy, you know, there are always setbacks in the early days – were effective for a while, because nobody wanted to admit that he might have made a dreadful mistake. But something more dramatic had to be done.

What was done was to request the auditors first to revalue the company's physical assets, and then, with Mr Keyser's skilled advice and encouragement, to write a recovery plan. A formula was found for revaluing the assets based on the use of current replacement value rather than depreciated historical cost, which had the happy event of increasing book values by over a million pounds. This gave the bank the security it needed to increase the overdraft limit by that amount. The recovery plan was equally ingenious and worked out in minute detail, based as always on the sanguine forecasts of raw material purchase prices and oil and meal sales prices provided by Julius Keyser. The rationale for the plan, requiring a further capital investment of £1.5 million, was twofold. The first argument was that if there were diseconomies in the relatively small scale of the company operations, the obvious remedy was to invest in further plant to double crushing capacity. The second argument was that the addition of refining capacity to the crushing capacity would add value to the product, eliminate the cost of shipping unrefined oil to distant refiners, and enable the end product to be sold locally. The combined effect of the two steps, with the increased output that would result, would be to spread fixed overheads more thinly and thus increase profits.

The backers were duly impressed, as they had hoped to be. The company was now approaching the end of its second year of business; turnover was increasing toward the plant's capacity limits, but the rate of loss was increasing at equal speed. Something needed to be done fast. Perhaps this final injection of capital would do the trick. However, before deciding to take the plunge, the authority and the bank took the precaution of inviting yet another firm of consultants to review the situation – this time with a wide brief and clear instructions to pull no punches.

The new marketing consultants took an exceptionally holistic view of the role of marketing, concerning themselves with the health of the entire organization and the long-term security of its niche in the marketplace. They wasted very little time on picking holes in the previous marketing consultants' market report (clearly they knew their business) or in checking the accountants' calculations (since they were accountants, their computerized calculations were almost certain to add up). Instead they stood back and took a quick overall look at the structure of the seed crushing industry, the continuing trend towards greater concentration and vertical integration, and the assumptions on which the calculations and conclusions were based. They looked particularly hard at the sensitivities on which the profitability of a small independent crushing mill would depend, in a market where there was already more than sufficient capacity. They were not happy with what they found – an essentially narrow profit margin, highly vulnerable to the much wider but independent price fluctuations of raw materials and end product.

Next they looked at the recommended solution of further investment in crushing capacity and the addition of oil refining capacity. There were some obvious fallacies in the rationale. More efficient use of the site and some improvement in the utilization of labour would not reduce unit costs very much; raw material and transport costs, plus the ever-growing cost of servicing borrowed capital, were much more important items. And the addition of refining capacity would complicate matters rather than reducing costs. Manufacturers of consumer products using vegetable oils normally expect to buy blended oils from the refinery, the blend varying according to their particular requirements and fluctuations in the prices of alternative oil seeds. So the captive refinery would need to buy in other oils to blend with the output of the crushing mill, thus reviving the original problem of high transportation costs and low buying power which it was designed to kill.

So what was to be done? Despite a professional urge to find a solution to every problem, the consultants could see no option. They advised the backers to cut their losses and the business was put into liquidation that weekend.

The saddest part about this sad story is that there are no heroes and no villains. Julius Keyser was not a villain. He enjoyed his new suit of clothes and would have been happy to see the business prosper so that he could continue wearing them indefinitely. The development authority and the bank were certainly not villains, though they could in the end have been accused of wishful thinking; they were genuinely anxious to play their part in solving the destructive and demoralizing problem of high unemployment. As for heroes, the firm's line management and operatives, who soldiered on while the business was falling around their ears, came closest to qualifying. Certainly the final consultants, who played the little boy role of revealing the Emperor's nakedness, did not regard

AND OF COURSE THERE'S VERY LITTLE COMPETITION ROUND HERE FROM OTHER PROPERTY DEVELOPERS..

themselves as heroes. Indeed they felt a certain chagrin that while the previous consultant had been paid in full, they themselves could only look forward to the probably very small percentage of their modest fee that the liquidator might eventually offer.

But it does suggest a number of new entries for the marketing commonplace book. For instance:

1 Don't go into a business where you'll always be out of your depth.
2 Look at the total picture in the long term, not just disassociated and temporary details.
3 Don't believe a project will succeed, just because you want it to.
4 Don't rush into a project, without adequate investigation, for fear that somebody else will get there first.
5 Don't believe anything you are told, particularly by interested parties, without independent checking.
6 Don't imagine you can buy your way out of a failure; it's better to cut your losses.
7 The marketing buck stops on the desk of the chief executive, not the marketing manager.

2 There's no such thing as marketing

There is a story, doubtless apocryphal, that the first professor of marketing at the London Business School was once heard to remark that in his considered opinion there is no such thing as marketing. This did not please those of his academic colleagues who looked forward to distinguished careers expounding the new science of marketing to the unenlightened.

From a practical viewpoint the professor, himself a very successful businessman, was right in what he said – if he ever said it. Marketing is not a self-contained discipline that produces results in isolation from the other managerial functions, such as production, purchasing, personnel and finance. It's a vital *management* function (if you can't market it, there's no point in making it) that needs to be skilfully blended with all the other functions that add up to a successful business.

Hence the saying coined by somebody or other (maybe it was me) that 'Marketing is too important to leave to the marketing men.' Hence also the grievous disappointment of so many boards of companies that had got along very nicely over the years without a distinct function called marketing, ran into problems of one kind or another (sometimes had no obvious problems, but had been told that marketing was all the rage these days), hired a marketing manager with a red hot reputation from some other industry (usually food or detergents), and sat back to wait for a rapid fire display of profitable conjuring tricks. Usually they waited in vain. Why?

It's dangerous to generalize in marketing or management matters; whatever assertion you make, the contrary, as the great Marx (Groucho) said, is also true. But several factors constantly recur in organizations that have accepted the importance of marketing in theory but failed to benefit from it in practice.

He's not one of us

You don't need to be an exceptionally perceptive observer of relationships in most management teams to recognize that beneath the surface there are intricate cross-currents of rivalries, jealousies, suspicions and misunderstandings. But there's nothing that unites the factions more rapidly than the arrival of a new character on the scene – particularly one who is not an engineer in an engineering firm, an accountant in a firm of accountants, a career banker in a bank, but simply claims to understand markets and customers.

There are many ways of putting the interloper in his place. He can be assigned to a remote office and left to his own devices. ('Ah yes, marketing,' says the chief executive to the enquiring visitor, 'we go in for a bit of that; you'd better have a word with young thingummy, my secretary will tell you where to find him.') You can exclude him from the meetings that really matter or starve him of information. Or you can instruct him to concentrate on market research, a relatively inexpensive and harmless pastime, as long as you take no action about the findings; it can be quite entertaining to read the reports and decide which of the findings you agree with and which you reject in the light of your established prejudices.

A particularly elegant method of sterilization was adopted by the sales manager of a consumer durable company, who welcomed a newly appointed marketing manager (recruited with an ambitious brief to change the company's business thrust from selling what the factory found it convenient to make towards marketing what the customer wanted) with open if insidious arms. 'You and I', said the sales manager, 'have clearly got to work together; after all, we both want the same thing – a satisfied customer. But we mustn't step on each other's toes. Tell you what – marketing's about planning for the future, right? And selling's about going out and getting the order today, right? So I'll be responsible for this year's sales plan and you'll be responsible for next year's marketing plan.'

The arrangement worked well for the rest of the year. The sales manager pursued his accustomed paths; and having been shrewd enough to publish sales forecasts rather lower than he and his men felt they could achieve, received his customary commendation from senior management for beating his targets. The marketing manager, meanwhile, was happy as a pig in clover, researching customer attitudes and behaviour, checking on changes in distribution channels and retailing methods, and observing the activities of competitors. He found a number of anomalies in the company's distributive pattern – great strength in certain sectors and comparative weakness in others, particularly in discount stores and new types of outlet which had recently grown in importance; he also found that the company was missing out on some of the merchandising techniques used by competitors, and that overall it was failing to hold its share of a rising market. He drafted a marketing plan for the following year, requiring significant changes in the deployment of the sales force and in sales promotional tactics, but promising considerably higher sales figures and profits if all went well.

Came the turn of the year, and the sales manager, secure in his vote of confidence from senior management, published his new year's sales plan – essentially 'Steady as you go.' 'But', protested the marketing manager, 'we agreed that I would write next year's plan; you're not playing fair.' 'What do you mean, not playing fair? It's not next year any more, it's this year, and I'm responsible.' In the ensuing management debate, the force of this logic, plus old established loyalties, carried the day.

Change – what, me?

Any marketing man worth his salt is obsessed with change. He sees the world around him changing with ever-increasing speed in its social, economic and political climate as well as its technological resources; and he becomes uneasy and frustrated when the organization for which he works fails to change as fast as the environment to which it must adapt if it is to survive.

But it is not in the nature of most men and women to welcome change, especially when they have achieved the comfort and dignity of senior management positions, where they can exercise the expertise they have built up over the years. It is easy enough to get heads nodding in agreement when you generalize about the inevitability of change and the need to review the product mix, seek new customers, and adopt new selling, distribution and ultimately production methods; there's always room for improvement in the way other people do their jobs. But when you move from the general to the particular and say that you the sales manager, you the production director, you the chief accountant, you the personnel director, yes and you the managing director must be the first to change, nodding heads start to shake alarmedly. Put another way, peripheral marketing in an organization where the powers that be are unwilling to accept the demands it makes on them as individuals is unlikely to get very far. It has to involve everybody who is anybody.

It won't work in this industry

This is a marketing repellent that deserves more respect than human inertia and reluctance to change. There have been cases where marketing techniques, transferred holus-bolus from one industry to another, have distorted the marketing effort of the transferee and done more harm than good. This happens all the more often because the still infant techniques of marketing (it is worth recalling that the first widely quoted academic statement on the subject, Theodore Levitt's article on marketing myopia, was only published in 1954) were originally developed in practice by American manufacturers of fast moving consumer goods like Procter & Gamble and General Foods. When industrial and service organiz-ations 'discovered' marketing rather later in the day, it was natural to think of it in terms of consumer product marketing – often indeed to recruit an alumnus of Procter & Gamble or some other consumer goods manufacturer to set up their new marketing departments.

All may be well if the individual concerned is capable of selective adaptation, shaping what he has learned in his old job to fit a new situation, and if his new colleagues enter into constructive dis-cussions about the practicalities. But only too often the individual, having been trained to follow a very rigid rulebook, assumes that what worked there will also work here; and his colleagues, impressed by his expert credentials, forbear to question the relevance of his expertise. Then there is trouble.

For the conditions and marketing priorities of, say, banking and packaged groceries are different. A bank aims to create a lifetime relationship with a customer in an area of fundamental importance to the latter's domestic economy; if the relationship goes wrong, the customer can be ruined. A detergent manufacturer's customer relationships are less serious; if little Johnny's shirt is not after all whiter than his friends', the customer buys another brand next week and the manufacturer improves the product, or if the worst comes to the worst, replaces it by another. Nobody, bankers included, will deny that there is room for improvement in the total relationship between bank and customer; but banks, having learned about marketing largely from advisers steeped in consumer product traditions, have spent most of their marketing effort up to now on launching a bewildering variety of packaged 'products' (far too many for consumers to assimilate) instead of concentrating on the improvement of basic relationships.

We can't produce it at that price

One of the skeletons rattling in my personal cupboard of marketing relics is the occasion long ago when I was involved in the launch of one of the first branded wines to hit the UK market. How long ago can be judged by the fact that at the time ten shillings was a considerable price for a bottle of plonk (ten shillings for the information of those whose memory does not stretch to pre-decimalization days, was the equivalent of 50p; and 50p then would be worth around £2.50 now).

A first-class advertising agency was briefed; it invented and researched a brand name and devised and researched an advertising campaign, complete with merchandising support material. A distribution plan was agreed. Just one crucial question remained – the price. We (marketing) and the sales force were certain that to be accepted by the big brewers – who then, as now, dominated retail liquor distribution – the new brand would have to be priced to retail below the then crucial price break of ten shillings. 'You may be right,' said company management, 'but if we are to sell at that price, it will have to be empty bottles; after the bottling, labelling, packaging, despatch and general management overheads, there'll be nothing left to pay for the wine.' 'But how do your competitors manage to do it?' 'Obviously, they don't have our overheads.'

That was the point at which we should have insisted that either the company found a way to get overheads down or it stayed out of this highly competitive market sector. Instead we accepted what we were told, on the grounds that it is not marketing's business to dig into costings, which are the province of production and accounts;

perhaps we would be lucky, even if the price was too high. We were not lucky; and we ceased to accept the assumption that costings are none of marketing's business. You can market a high-priced product if it is also of high quality; but no marketing magic will get away for long with a product that is not value for money. Production and accounts must be persuaded to join the marketing team.

We can't let our old customers down

Pareto's law, to the effect that 80 per cent of most companies' business comes from 20 per cent of its customers, is too well known – and too inevitable – to be laboured. What is less frequently remarked is that in many organizations which have lacked tight marketing and financial control, at least 20 per cent of the customers are being handled at a loss; and at least 20 per cent of potentially profitable customers are not being contacted at all.

Correcting this situation should be a straightforward marketing task. Just tell the unprofitable customers that they will have to pay more or shop elsewhere; and start courting the potentially profitable ones. But, of course, it is not that easy. Old friendships and loyalties are involved; and the potentially profitable new customers will also be loyal to their existing suppliers and may not be readily wooed and won. Courage and senior management support will be needed to embark on the transition and endure the temporary loss of turnover (though not necessarily of profits) that may result.

And before that, reliable cost figures will be needed to prove beyond a peradventure which are the profitable and which the unprofitable customers.

It's profitable, because I say it is

This leads to the point that marketing is at best futile and at worst disastrous, if you don't have reliable financial figures with which to estimate the likely consequences of the choices you make and to measure the results of your actions. The innocent marketing man, adrift in a company with an unsatisfactory cost accounting system and inadequate facilities for making special analyses of sensitive areas (unhappily there are many such), is always at risk. Sooner or later he will find that the profit figures he was trained to lean on and steer by are not fixed points at all, but can be changed at the accountants' whim; and he is floating rudderless on an uncharted sea. The activity he is responsible for is profitable, or not, because the accountant says so.

One of the earliest UK companies to adopt the principle of profit-responsible product management was, unsurprisingly, American owned – and heavily supervised from across the Atlantic. I was privileged at one time to attend the annual visitations of the international vice-president, at which the young product group managers (PGMs) presented their results for the previous year and their plans for the year to come. The annual event, though never televised, became in the end a sort of beauty contest, absorbing far more of the product groups' time and merchandising budgets than purely commercial considerations required.

For several years it was Don F. who was crowned Mr PGM. Not only was he an exceptionally fluent presenter and manipulator of visual aids, but his profit ratios invariably came closest to the very demanding standards set by the transatlantic parent. Invariably, that is, until the year when profit contributions suddenly turned to loss. There was no mystery about the reason. Nothing very much had changed in the marketplace; his products had more than held their market share. It was just that the accounts department had changed the system for allocating overheads and Don's products had been clobbered. The glissade from top of the class to bottom, however, was too much for him and shortly thereafter he accepted a job in another company – in which he prospered exceedingly, having learnt the lesson that marketing cannot live without the active involvement of financial control.

Organizational constipation

It is fair to say that no human organization involving more than two people runs so smoothly that no energy is dissipated in friction. But there are some forms of organization which make it almost impossible for the person or persons responsible for marketing to discharge their appointed task of promoting change. A glaring example is the decentralized organization where marketing is positioned as a staff function alongside other staff functions at the centre, vainly attempting to guide the marketing activities of highly independent, profit-responsible general managers of divisions or managing directors of subsidiaries.

Ralph Halpern, one of a small number of big company chief executives who is himself an outstanding marketing man, found such a situation when he took over command of the Burton Tailoring Group, a concern that had known for years that it needed to change in order to survive in a radically changed market but had failed in its attempts to do so until bankruptcy was just around the corner.

Halpern's cure for the organization's stubborn constipation was to decree that in future there would be no general managers in the divisions, just functional managers reporting to functional bosses at the centre. This worked in Burton's, as part of a wider plan. It might not work so well in other companies where the divisions or subsidiaries are self-contained businesses, too diverse to be fully understood at the centre. In such cases the marketing function would be better located in the operating divisions. There is no golden rule except that marketing, if it is to produce profits and not just papers, needs to be where the action is and where the decisions are taken.

It would be going too far to suggest that a newly appointed head of marketing should start by lobbying to change the organization in which he works. But often marketing skills and expenditure are wasted because the organization does not permit them to operate effectively – another justification for the statement that marketing involves more than the marketing men.

The tyranny of time

Most managements, very properly, are concerned with profit; if they aren't, their shareholders will quickly draw it to their attention. Moreover, it is usually a short-term concern. The pressure is on a company that did badly last year to do better this year, and on a company that did well this year to do even better next year.

This can be a cause of some embarrassment to marketers, who are equally concerned with profit, but can seldom deliver it as fast by the growth and diversification road that is their primary route as can the accountants by cost-cutting. There is usually room for cost reduction in marketing, for instance by axing unprofitable products or customers; and it is only prudent to eliminate any waste before asking for additional funds. But marketing innovation more often than not is a question of jam tomorrow, with the bill having to be paid today. It has to be a general management decision – one that it requires some courage to sustain – to invest a proportion of this year's profits not simply in tangible assets, but in the creation of future business. It requires conscientiousness as well as courage if the executives concerned benefit from profit-sharing bonuses, and are likely to be retired by the time the marketing investment pays off.

Macro-marketing versus micro-marketing

It can be helpful sometimes to distinguish between those business development questions which are part of the overall management task of matching resources to opportunities and can be described as strategic or macro-marketing, and those which do not require fundamental changes and can be described as micro-marketing. The head of marketing can be directly responsible for the latter, but cannot expect to play more than a contributory, though important, role in the former.

Macro-marketing questions that should concern every member of the management team start with the old but still meaty chestnut, 'What business are we in?' – more pertinently, 'How is that business changing?' and 'What problems/opportunities do predictable changes involve?' It may be, for example, that some of the organization's traditional activities are no longer appropriate; or that new technology must be taken aboard; or that the organization is not large enough to survive alone in a competitive international market. All of management should be concerned to know who are the company's customers, actual and potential, and how far their needs are being satisfied. All should be keeping a wary eye on competitors, to make sure that there's *something* of importance to some customers that the company does better (you can't hope to do everything better than everybody). All should be concerned about deploying the organization's people resources to the best effect (most individuals in most companies are visibly contributing less than they are willing and able to do). They should, of course, be concerned about utilizing the organization's capital resources to the best effect. And, having decided what they want or need to do, they should all be concerned about how the devil to pay for it.

The head of marketing should, if the organization and internal relationships permit, be able to contribute evidence and constructive ideas to the solution of these macro-marketing questions. Clear-cut answers and decisive action in the strategic area, apart from anything else, will make it very much easier for him to handle the micro-marketing matters for which he should be directly responsible. These include such questions as: How do we get more customers? How do we increase our business with existing customers? How can we improve the acceptability of our products? How can we improve our reputation with target customers and opinion formers? How can we increase the cost-effectiveness of our selling and distributive organization? How can we get better value for our promotional expenditure? What should be our pricing policy? How can we increase the understanding of marketing principles in all members of the organization and their active involvement in turning principles into practice?

Entries for the chief executive's diary

If a marketing adviser's fairy godmother gave him the chance to plant seven entries in a chief executive's diary, he would probably choose a list like this:

1 The marketing buck stops at your desk.
2 Where the business will be in ten years' time is more important than where it is today.
3 It's up to you to set the pace and direction of organizational change. . .
4 And to get all the pieces and all the people working smoothly together in achieving it.
5 'If you don't experiment you can't accumulate.' Take *controlled* risks and accept a proportion of failures.
6 Know your own strength. Pick marketing battlegrounds where you have a good chance of winning.

7 'Yond Cassius has a lean and hungry look; / He thinks too much: such men are dangerous.' But it's useful to have the odd Cassius around if you want to stay ahead in a competitive world. Men who are fat resist change.

3 A touch of the Machiavellis

It must be considered that there is nothing more difficult, more dangerous or more apt to miscarry than an endeavour to introduce new institutions. For he that introduces them will make enemies of all those who do well out of the old institutions, and will receive only cool support from those who would do well out of the new ones. This coolness is caused partly by fear of their opponents, who have the old laws on their side, and partly from the natural scepticism of mankind, who have no faith in new arrangements until they have been confirmed by experience.

(Machiavelli, *The Prince*, Chapter 6)

Machiavelli, with his shrewd grasp of what makes people tick, would have made an excellent marketing consultant. Indeed *The Prince* was a sales pitch to the Medicis for some such role, which unfortunately failed to land the job; Machiavelli got arrested and tortured instead. (Few recalcitrant clients are quite so disagreeable nowadays.)

But successful or not, he was right about the difficulty of bringing about change in any established organization and indeed about the danger (in career terms) of being identified as the apostle of change. On the other hand, marketing is all about change – anticipating or at least reacting to changes in market conditions, consumer demand and the knavish devices of competitors. A marketing man who sits back and accepts the status quo is not worth his salt. It's better to be awkward and uncomfortable than ineffectual.

In the end a marketer at any level who wants to achieve results not only must be a capable technician, but needs to practise some of the manipulative skills in human relations that Machiavelli expounds. In America, where the stark choice between using people and being used is accepted more openly than in England, Richard Christie has developed a 'Machiavelli test' to measure the extent to which individuals are temperamentally attuned to the manipulation of their fellows (whether for good reasons or for bad). You get a high Mach score if you favour telling people what they want to hear, don't completely trust anybody, cut corners if you have to, assume that everybody has a vicious streak, only reveal your real reasons if it's useful to do so, flatter the people who matter, find euthanasia acceptable, and believe that property matters more than people, that people are naturally lazy, that it's the stupid criminal who gets caught and that a sucker's born every minute; and if you discount the views that you should give your real reasons, that honesty is the best policy, that you should act only when you are sure it's morally right, that it's better to be humble and honest than important and dishonest, that it's possible to be good in all respects, and that most people are good, kind and brave, lead moral lives and don't tell lies.

For those who are curious about their own Mach scores, the Machiavelli test questionnaire can be found at the end of this chapter. Anybody who scores maximum marks will either be a monster or cheating; those who honestly record a high score may hate themselves for it, but will probably have at least one of the main qualifications for success in marketing management; for those whose scores are really low, it may not yet be too late to enter holy orders.

Preach the gospel or get results?

Like all theories, the machiavellian doctrine needs to be taken with a pinch of salt; too obvious an attempt to manipulate colleagues or customers is likely to offend to a greater or lesser degree, depending on the culture of the organization concerned. In some organizations the internal battle for power is naked and unashamed, in others it is concealed beneath a gentlemanly veneer, in others again it is said that there are no conflicts but everybody works harmoniously together for the common good; I confess that I have yet to meet any in the third category.

Whatever the situation, a marketer who finds himself in an

organization where the kind of changes that marketing requires are faced by human as well as practical resistances must choose whether to preach the pure marketing gospel (and risk a fiery end, like Savaronola's at the stake) or modify doctrine for the sake of getting results.

This was the dilemma that faced two very able marketers of my acquaintance, both of whom were recruited at much the same time out of consumer product marketing by financial service companies, whose managements believed that they would benefit from a dose of marketing. Let us call them Bill and Ben, the marketing men.

William B. Carmody – Bill to his rather restricted circle of friends – was recruited by the Blue Sky Insurance Company with a distinctly imprecise brief to prepare the company for difficult times ahead by building a professional marketing department on the skimpy foundations laid by the existing advertising manager and research manager. He felt more than equal to the assignment, having obtained a wide, if not always deep, experience of marketing organization in one of those meteoric careers favoured by young upwardly mobile marketing executives (two or three years with a top advertising agency, another two or three years with a leading packaged goods company, and then on to the next job).

He made an auspicious start. Nobody was prepared to say a word against marketing, since management had decreed that henceforward the company would be led by marketing; and Bill Carmody was the appointed leader. When he asked for the advertising budget to be quadrupled, this was agreed with little demur; and the new campaign, devised by the newly appointed advertising agency, was much admired in the trade. He initiated a much more vigorous PR campaign, directed particularly at brokers, whose collective noses had been put seriously out of joint the year before when the company had announced a policy of direct selling which had not been wholly successful. He commissioned an elaborate and costly attitude research study, which revealed that the company's image was far from satisfactory; on the strength of this he persuaded a now uneasy management – who did not like the news that their customers had neither love nor respect for them – that more money should be spent on image-building advertising. He pointed out that the company's range of policies had a number of gaps when compared with those of competitors, and hired a product development agency to devise additional packages with guaranteed consumer appeal. He worked out new sales targets for the branches, based on the calculated potential of their catchment areas rather than the existing system whereby branch managers set their own targets – with some encouragement from district managers when they were too cautious. And he organized a national marketing conference, where managers were assembled from around the country to be lectured on the theory of marketing.

All of this cost a great deal of money and also necessitated the rapid construction of a large central marketing department. But as Bill was frequently heard to observe, you can't make an omelette without breaking eggs. Nevertheless it was imprudent to do it all quite so fast. More imprudent, in the light of subsequent events, were some of the things Bill failed to do. He failed to monitor the results of his marketing initiatives or to relate expenditure to putative return. He failed to get out and around the branches, in order to gather a first-hand impression of the day-to-day marketing problems they were struggling with, and to convey the impression that he was eager to help them. He failed to listen to the advice of the advertising and research managers he had inherited; they were no great shakes as marketing technicians, but were wise in the ways of the company and could have warned him of the growing resistance movement. Worst of all, he was arrogant and let it be known that he had very little respect for the commercial acumen of the company's senior managers and power brokers.

Also he was unlucky. The good that he did on the marketing side of the business (and it was considerable) was heavily outweighed in the two years of his incumbency by an unprecedented succession of fires, floods, fogs and hurricanes, resulting in heavy underwriting losses. The opponents of marketing, the resisters of change and the enemies of Bill Carmody were able to demonstrate, with impeccably flawed logic, that the only clear result of the heavy investment in marketing had been ruffled feelings and reduced profits. The point was taken; Bill departed with only a modest golden handshake; and life became peaceful – though not more profitable – once again.

Ben Donne had much the same provenance as Bill Carmody. He too had worked with a packaged goods company and an advertising agency. But he had then had a spell in marketing consultancy, where he handled assignments for industrial as well as consumer goods companies and observed the differences between them in marketing approach; he also observed the different ways in which the then less familiar tool of computerization was used or misused for marketing purposes. He was attracted by the opportunity when the new management of London and Provincial Bank, one of the smaller national banking groups, offered him the job of setting up their new marketing department; he was even more attracted by their statement that 'As a relatively small bank we have to be better at something, and we've decided to be better at marketing – whatever that may mean.'

Ben was a cautious character; some might call him devious or even machiavellian. He recognized very rapidly that London and Provincial were deficient in much the same marketing attributes as Blue Sky Insurance; they lacked a sound body of market research on which to base their development strategy, their products were insufficiently differentiated from their competitors', and their advertising was still of the tombstone variety, much favoured at the time by bankers (the much derided advertisement of the banker emerging coyly from the cupboard under the stairs had yet to be devised). He set to work to remedy these deficiencies *over time*, pacing the rate of change and expenditure levels to keep step with the organization's ability to absorb and exploit them.

Meanwhile Ben worked on developing a sales forecasting model, for planning rather than sales targeting purposes. A reliable forecast of incremental sales revenue would, he reckoned, help him to justify the increased marketing budget he was likely to need; whereas any attempt to set individual branch targets, related to global objectives, was better left to line managers who had the disciplinary clout that he lacked. He also worked hard and successfully to persuade senior management that as a small bank, with more flexibility and more to gain than their competitors, they could afford to make greater use of the price weapon (through 'free' banking and so on) in attracting new customers. This could, and in the event did, mean that the bank's market share would be seen to increase – a useful step down the road of building credibility for this thing called marketing.

By concentrating on the essentials and recruiting a slim team of well-qualified assistants to whom he could delegate, Ben made time for himself to get out and around the branches. This was useful not only in converting him from a signature at the foot of marketing circulars into a living, talking head, but also in identifying the problems and opportunities involved in the development of the bank's core business at branch level. (One of the criticisms that could be levelled at bank marketing in the early days was that it concentrated overmuch on the promotion of peripheral services like insurance and investment management, paying insufficient attention to the core problem of attracting deposits from the public.) Ben Donne found that few of the branch managers he visited had adequately researched the business potential of their catchment areas, or worked out systematic plans either for developing more business among their existing customers or for reaching the best prospects among non-customers. He assigned two of his bright young assistants to work with half a dozen guinea-pig branches on preparing localized business development plans, including provision for monitoring results; and to package the procedure they had adopted into a DIY manual for the use of other branch managers. As the evidence of success came in from the guinea-pig branches, other managers, urged on by their regional managers, were encouraged to set forth down the do-it-yourself road. The word travelled up the managerial grapevine that marketing was not all textbook theory and Ben was a useful chap to have on board – even to involve in planning the bank's corporate strategy.

Of course, as he is prepared to admit now that he is a fully paid up member of senior management, Ben Donne was lucky. The banking industry was going through a prosperous phase during his early years, with any loss of business to building societies and other competitors compensated by market growth and high interest rates. But he deserved to be lucky because he was realistic about timing and about the need to establish credibility before attempting to procure major changes in marketing attitudes and methods.

The marketing Machiavelli

A marketing man who is appointed chief executive may not need to worry overmuch about the art of manipulating others – though even the supreme commander has shareholders and bankers to consider, as well as subordinates, and persuasion in the long run may get further with the latter than unadorned directives.

But anywhere below the top, the effective marketer must supplement his technical skills with the art of persuading or manoeuvring the people involved in carrying out his projects into changing their attitudes and behaviour. One of the main rules of marketing is that there are no unbreakable rules; but there are some which should only be broken with very good reason.

The easy break-it-at-your-peril rules for the recruited or promoted marketer, with a mission to sharpen the marketing thrust of an organization, are the organizational and procedural ones. The most important are:

Get yourself a budget   It is not uncommon for managements, having nerved themselves to accept the outrageous salary commanded by a marketer with a good track record, to baulk at the budget needed to achieve results. Brilliant as he may be, mountains cannot be moved without a fund to buy the dynamite.

Hire your own advertising and PR agencies   However good the existing incumbents – they will never be so good that you cannot pick holes in their performance – their loyalty will be to the past. You need supporters who will share your anxiety to make changes (let's hope for the better) and whose first loyalty will be to you.

Establish good relations with accounts   This is not just a question of getting your departmental expense accounts approved – though there is no harm in that. It is much more fundamentally a matter of positioning marketing as a *profit-oriented business activity*, rather than an expensive luxury which can be chopped when times get hard.

Establish good relations with personnel   Unless the organization is very small, the effectiveness of its marketing thrust will ultimately depend more on the behaviour, attitudes and priorities of many individuals at all levels than on the single-handed efforts of the marketing supremo. If personnel management understands this and is willing to co-operate, its help will be invaluable in three areas: first, in recognizing that as the marketing department builds up it will need to be staffed by people of exceptional drive and initiative, not by misfits from other departments; second, in including marketing modules in training programmes for all members of staff coming directly or indirectly into contact with customers; and third, in making explicit provision in the individual performance assessment system for attainments in the area of customer service and business development.

Weed out unprofitable products and customers   Provided that you have better uses for the resources released in this way, ceasing to serve customers or support products that cost the company money can be the shortest route to the increased profits that give credibility to marketing. The weeding out needs to be done in a way that avoids ill will. Products can be killed by raising prices and withdrawing promotional support (sometimes they refuse to die and linger on into a highly profitable though dwindling old age). Customers can be handed over to stockists or wholesalers, or can be asked to pay the real cost of servicing them. Either way, you create tactical and budgetary elbow room.

Spend time in the field with branch managers and salesmen   The image of an ivory tower theoretician, issuing textbook directives, will get you nowhere; and the directives will probably be wide of the mark. There will be a lot of repetition about these field trips, and you may sometimes feel you are wasting your time. But if you are prepared to listen, you will find out what the real problems are; and when you ask for support you will be a person, not just the signature at the bottom of yet another head office circular.

Build on what's already being done well   Usually you will find a lot of marketing things being done well, if sporadically and un-systematically, in an organization that supposedly has never heard of marketing. It's better to build on and systematize these things, giving them a new slant where necessary, than to play the new broom and sweep the good away with the bad.

Gain credibility by quick pay-off projects   In the long run, what the organization probably needs is a major shift in marketing direction or method. But in the long run we are all dead – including you, the highly suspect advocate of change. While you are incubating the major changes, which will take time and cost money, it is prudent to demonstrate that marketing can produce results by initiating some highly visible, uncontroversial short-term projects.

But don't get so bogged down in these projects that you lose sight of the broader issues.

Keep your departmental team slim The trend in employment nowadays – making the unemployment problem no easier – is towards fewer, more productive employees. Fewer operatives on the factory floor, backed by robots and computer-controlled plant; fewer salesmen, concentrating on key accounts; and fewer but larger retail outlets. You will be well advised to follow this trend in the marketing department, surrounding yourself with a few well-qualified individuals who can support you in preaching the marketing faith rather than building a mini-empire, exposed to the chop in any economy drive.

The more machiavellian people-related rules are harder to follow, because they depend on the personality of the individual attempting to follow them. If that's simply not the kind of person you are, there's no point in trying to fake it. But these rules are worth considering:

Identify and make friends with the power brokers The people whose support is vital for securing acceptance of the marketing concept may not be those who appointed you, professing unreserved confidence in the importance of marketing. They may have been predestined losers in the corporate power game, hoping that a new factor would somehow shift the balance in their favour. Becoming too closely identified with any faction is unwise. The proper Machiavelli will convince all concerned that his marketing machinations will further their particular interests – and if they make the business more prosperous, they probably will.

Recruit some insiders to teach you the corporate language The temptation to build up a department by recruiting marketing specialists only from outside the organization should be resisted. You will need one or two insiders, who may be deficient in marketing expertise but have observed the way things get done in the organization, to advise you on the intricacies of internal politicking.

Get a reputation for helpfulness Ben Donne's approach of first persuading branch managers to let him operate a business development project on their behalf and then encouraging others to do it themselves with his advice could be an interesting precedent to follow, where conditions permit. Half the point of field trips is to discover localized problems you can help to solve.

Give others the credit for the successes   This is not a question of altruism, just enlightened self-interest. If you are going to make things happen, you need all the supporters you can muster; and people whose reputation you enhance will be stronger supporters than those on whose backs you climb. Eventually the word will get around that you seem to carry success with you.

Keep people interested and informed   People co-operate better when they feel interested and involved; and fortunately marketing is an interesting subject. So internal communications deserve a lot of creative thought; it's a more serious matter than simply sending a copy to everybody you can think of, whenever you commit yourself to paper.

Be realistic about timing   Changing people's attitudes and behaviour takes a frustratingly long time, unless there is some strong motivating factor such as fear – and people are seldom at their best when they are frightened. If the climate is really cold and the organization about to go bust, you will be able (and need) to move fast. If not, you will probably have to restrain yourself and adopt a tempo that the organization can tolerate. An anti-marketing backlash is always a hazard for those like Bill Carmody who lack patience and, if you will, deviousness.

Oh, in expounding the machiavellian rulebook I almost forgot: if you have any time to spare from all the political manoeuvring that is essential to get results, do try to fit in a spot of advertising, product development and market research.

Human relationships' questionnaire

The following questions ask you about how you behave at work, what you believe about human relationships, and what values you place on them.

Each question is presented as a statement, and you are asked to choose one of seven possible responses:

Strongly agree (SA)
Somewhat agree (SWA)
Slightly agree (SLA)
No opinion (N/O)
Slightly disagree (SLD)
Somewhat disagree (SWD)
Strongly disagree (SD)

There are no right or wrong answers, so please be as honest as you can.

Question	SA	SWA	SLA	N/O	SLD	SWD	SD
1 The best way to handle people is to tell them what they want to hear.							
2 When you ask someone to do something for you, it is best to give the real reasons rather than reasons which might carry more weight.							
3 Anyone who completely trusts anyone else is asking for trouble.							
4 It is hard to get ahead without cutting corners here and there.							
5 Honesty is the best policy.							
6 It is safest to assume that all people have a vicious streak and it will come out given a chance.							
7 Never tell anyone the real reason you did something unless it is useful to do so.							
8 You should take action only when you are sure it is morally right.							
9 It is wise to flatter important people.							

	SA	SWA	SLA	N/O	SLD	SWD	SD
10 All in all, it is better to be humble and honest than important and dishonest.							
11 Barnum was very wrong when he said there's a sucker born every minute.							
12 People suffering from incurable diseases should have the choice of being put painlessly to death.							
13 It is possible to be good in all respects.							
14 Most people are basically good and kind.							
15 There is no excuse for lying to someone else.							
16 Most people forget more easily the death of a parent than the loss of their property.							
17 Most people who get ahead in the world live clean, moral lives.							
18 Generally speaking, people won't work hard unless they're forced to do so.							
19 The biggest difference between most criminals and other people is that the criminals are stupid enough to get caught.							
20 Most people are brave.							

Notes

This questionnaire is also known as the Machiavelli test: it measures machiavellian tendencies. It was developed by Richard Christie in New York, and considerable research has been done using the test. It is surprisingly effective in predicting whether a person becomes emotionally involved with other people, or simply uses them for his own ends.

Males are generally more machiavellian than females, despite popular belief to the contrary! People in the 'manipulative' professions, such as lawyers, teachers and nurses, score more highly than those in the passive professions, like accountancy or science. People with high Mach scores are better at coping with uncertainty.

Machiavellianism does not appear to be related to other psychological traits, such as intelligence or extroversion. People with high intelligence are not thereby any more or less machiavellian than their less bright colleagues.

However, if they are machiavellian, their intelligence helps. Some British research reported by John Touhey in the *British Journal of Social and Clinical Psychology* seems to show that the right mixture of intelligence and machiavellianism can be important in ensuring that you get on in life. Touhey looked at a group of 120 men who, compared with their fathers, had either risen or gone down in the world. He found that those who had gone up, with better paid, socially more desirable jobs, had high scores on both IQ and Mach tests; whereas those who had gone down had equally high Mach scores, but much lower IQ scores. So a high score on this test will give you a high machiavellian tendency – but beware you don't overstrain your intelligence!

Scoring key

Question numbers:	SA	SWA	SLA	N/O	SLD	SWD	SD
1, 3, 4, 6, 7, 9, 12, 16, 18, 19:	7	6	5	4	3	2	1
2, 5, 8, 10, 11, 13, 14, 15, 17, 20:	1	2	3	4	5	6	7

Calculate your overall total score, and then add 20 to get your Mach score:

Overall total:

+ 20
_____

Mach score:

The range of scores is 40 to 160. The mean score for British managers is 96 and for American managers is 100. Scores over 120 are high on political behaviour; under 90 are low.

4 Creating a customer

'There is only one valid definition of business purpose: to create a customer,' as Peter Drucker has written in *Management: Tasks, Responsibilities, Practices* (Heinemann). Innumerable managers at countless management courses have absorbed this well-worn quotation over the years and few have disputed it; nobody can deny that without a customer you haven't got a business.

But what you are told on courses or read in books is one thing; what you do in real life is another. And the real life preoccupation of most managers is not with customers but with cash flow, cost control, sales targets, production schedules, how to frustrate the nefarious designs of their esteemed colleagues, how to achieve their own personal ambitions. Whoever in the management team carries the torch for marketing (in the best case it will be the chief executive, in the worst a lonely character whom nobody loves churning out market reports that nobody reads) has the difficult task of distracting the attention of functional managers from exclusive concentration on the activities described in their job specifications towards calculation of the effect of those activities on customers.

In theory nothing could be easier. You commission market research to establish relevant customer needs. You design a product range, or it may be a range of services, to satisfy those needs. You price your products so as to give the customer a reasonable bargain while giving the company an adequate profit return for its efforts. You use the very best promotional tools to let the lucky customer know what a bargain he is getting, and to let your colleagues and financiers know what a good thing you are on to. After that, it's just a question of keeping the ball rolling, in the best of all possible worlds.

But this isn't a world in which things go smoothly. The first thing the innocent marketer finds, when he starts to apply his business school principles, is that the sums don't add up. The price customers are prepared to pay for the ideal products or services your research has defined does not compare at all favourably with the cost the company accountants have worked out for producing, delivering and paying the appropriate share of corporate overheads on the sales volume you have projected; instead of a comfortable positive gap, labelled profit, there is a negative gap. What is worse, the escape route of saying 'Then they'll just have to pay more' is blocked by the unaccountable fact that competitors are managing to supply a product looking very like your ideal, below the accountants' calculated cost for producing and distributing your product.

So, unless he is prepared to abandon his ideas and start again, with probably no better chance of getting the sums right, the marketer is forced to evacuate his ivory tower and do battle with the accountants and production people. If the competitors can earn a profit at a lower price, why can't we? If overheads are too high, cannot they be reduced? If labour costs are too high, cannot productivity be increased, through better training, supervision, performance incentives and so on? If a larger competitor benefits from economies of scale, cannot this be countered by investment in more modern, specialized plant?

Alternatively, if costs are irredeemably high, cannot some element of uniqueness be built into the product or service to justify a higher price? A product, for example, can be engineered to fit in more closely with the production processes of customers or a definable group of customers, or to be more easily maintained. A service, as any beleaguered householder will testify, can always be improved by the old-fashioned virtues of speed, efficiency and courtesy – some of which need not increase costs.

But inevitably, once a marketing man gets into the practicalities of creating a customer, and starts to ask awkward questions, he will be accused of having ideas above his station, of trespassing outside the boundaries of his acknowledged expertise in market research, development planning, customer communications and promotion; jurisdictional disputes inevitably loom up. You are forced to the conclusion that if marketing is to deliver results, either the marketing man must be a business man and a manager, with substantial clout in the organization; or the chief executive must himself assume the ultimate responsibility for marketing, with such help as he needs from marketing technicians.

Market segmentation

The marketing task of creating a customer is not just a matter of persuading a proportion, large or small, of a featureless aggregation of potential customers to be reasonable, see it your way, accept your proposition and buy your product; it is much more a question of developing a dialogue, ideally over a long period, between a recognizable band of customers whose needs are understood, and a supplier prepared to go to some trouble to satisfy those needs. Both sides have to make concessions if the dialogue is to prosper. But, barring a monopoly, the supplier's concessions will have to be greater; customers can all seek alternative suppliers, while suppliers can't get along without customers. Even suppliers of inter-changeable mass market products like soap powder find that a hard core of *loyal* customers is invaluable, accounting for a dispro-portionately large share of total sales.

If it were not for the marketing technique of *market segment-*

ation, the possibility of creating a long-term dialogue with a loyal band of customers would be greatly reduced; given the heterogeneity of human needs and circumstances, you cannot hope to be all things to all men. Without segmentation, conscious or accidental, the chances of new companies or new products successfully penetrating markets dominated by a few powerful suppliers would be even slimmer than they already are.

In its simplest terms (it's not a particularly complicated concept) market segmentation requires you to select a manageable segment of the market, where your product or service has a potential advantage, in at least some respects, over competitors; and then focus your product development and promotional efforts on satisfying the needs of that segment. If, for example, you are ill-advised enough to own a village store, you know to begin with that you cannot compete either in variety of stock or in average price with the chain supermarket in the nearby town. So, after wondering whether you wouldn't be better off driving the school bus, you settle down to consider what you can offer that the supermarket cannot and who is likely to be interested in your offerings.

You will probably conclude that the most obvious benefits you can offer, to compensate for your higher price and lower choice, are the conveniences of time and place; local shoppers do not need to take the car or catch the bus to the market town; and with no unions to pacify, you can keep later opening hours. Add a telephone ordering and delivery service, having costed them out to make sure they are affordable, and you have the beginnings of a different 'product', which may even seem a better product to some people some of the time – to those within walking distance and without a car perhaps most of the time, to those needing to top up their weekly supermarket purchases perhaps some of the time.

What more can you do to enhance your product difference? Offer credit? Better be careful; it could be risky and expensive, particularly when your carless customers are unlikely to have much in the bank. Publicize competitions, promotions and price offers organized by your wholesalers or manufacturers? Make sure that, unlike green stamps, they don't take away a chunk of your already slender profit margin, and then splash them; they will demonstrate that the supermarket is not the only place to get a bargain or the chance of a bonanza. Maintain a friendly atmosphere? That could be important. A supermarket is an impersonal and usually un-friendly place; economics will drive you towards self-selection, if not the full rigours of self-service, but at least you can provide some help and advice to shoppers, recognize them by name, move some way towards becoming the social centre for the village – and train your help to adopt the right mix of friendliness and salesmanship.

Also, having begun to define and recognize your target customer segments, you can organize your inevitably limited stock to appeal to them. For the less affluent unmotorized segment you may have to think in terms of the lower end of the grocery product range, and either of giant economy packs or more likely of small packs where a low unit price compensates for relatively poor value; for the rich farmers' wives and cottage gentry you may look for your product difference in fresh home-baked bread, health foods or, if you can find a good cook in the neighbourhood, in ready-to-serve delicatessen items at the weekend. And of course you will need a tempting display of sweeties – not too easily snitched – for the junior pocket-money brigade. If you have observed the marketing principle of measurement and set up a simple stock control mechanism you should be able to experiment with different lines, different display positions, and different days of the week for featuring delicatessen or other special items.

Define your target customer segments, define your product proposition; next in the process of creating a customer (an unending process, if you have the vital urge constantly to experi-ment and improve) comes the familiar marketing activity of telling people about it. That's a matter of the medium and the message. The message must be interesting enough to catch people's attention with the most attention-catching notion of all, 'There could be something in it for me.' The medium or media must be selective enough to reach the target customer segments without also reaching so many irrelevant people that the cost is out of proportion to the results. Advertising even in the local paper will probably be unaffordable for this reason. But perhaps it will be feasible to arrange for leaflets or, much better, personally addressed letters to be delivered with the newspapers in the immediate neighbourhood, inviting people to product demonstrations or other special events. Perhaps you can use window displays and stickers to attract the passing trade. Admittedly the fashion in self-service and self-selection is for displays to be inward-looking rather than outward-looking, but you can do better than the friendly neighbourhood shopkeeper of my acquaintance who filled his window with precariously balanced mountains of toilet paper to discourage Peeping Toms – and wondered why he attracted so few passers-by. Perhaps you will not be too modest to promote yourself as the symbol of your shop, becoming a pillar of the community, giving cookery demonstrations at the village hall, organizing raffles and so on, all with a commercial as well as an altruistic end in mind.

The basis for market segmentation will, of course, be more complex in more complicated businesses – not that running a profitable village store is all that simple. Depending on the size and character of a business, its target market can be segmented geographically, making it possible for a relatively small company with short lines of communication to compete with much larger companies in a defined region or country; this can be particularly relevant with bulky products, where transport costs are high in relation to value. Or the market can be segmented by distribution channel, when a company elects to specialize in selling direct to customers or to concentrate on building relationships with a designated type or level of distributor. Or the market for a product with applications in a variety of industries can be segmented by industry, with the totality of marketing effort, from research and product design to sales representation, promotion and servicing facilities, focused on satisfying the needs of that industry.

When it comes to segmenting individual customers into bite-size chunks, the available options are considerable, though seldom definitive. The obvious ones like age, sex (avoiding sexism), occupation and income group are convenient because most standard market research studies are designed so that these classifications can be broken out separately or in combination; if you want to isolate the attitudes and behaviour of upper-income teenage girls you can do so (though the subsample you get may be too small to mean much).

But other segments, though not always so easily defined, may be more relevant to particular products or services. One not very helpful form of segmentation, hallowed by long use in market research, is the grandiloquently titled *socio-economic status*. Roughly speaking this means that if you look prosperous and talk proper you are classified as group AB; if you or your spouse are in some moderately well-paid non-manual occupation you are classified as group C1, or if manual and less well-paid group C2; if you are unemployed, an old-age pensioner or otherwise underprivileged you are dumped into group DE, a segment of little interest to those with something to sell.

Socio-economic segmentation worked well enough when the officer class was prosperous and the other ranks were not; and it helped market research interviewers, stopping people in the street and assigning them on sight to one or other group. But the internal compatibility of the term 'socio-economic' becomes increasingly irreconcilable as society gets more mobile. How do you classify in socio-economic terms an Oxford-educated curate and a semi-literate pop singer?

A more practical form of segmentation for commercial purposes is by *lifestyle*, as manifested in possessions and leisure activities. Whether or not a family has its own home, a car or cars, a garden, a telephone, an audiovisual recorder, whether holidays are taken abroad or in a caravan, the extent of educational and sporting interests, are all ascertainable factors, of positive or negative significance depending on the product or service you have it in mind to market.

Life cycle is another form of segmentation of special interest to organizations like banks and insurance companies – and governments – seeking to establish cradle-to-grave relationships with individuals. Following in the footsteps of Shakespeare's seven ages of man, the life cyclists usually distinguish six main segments. Children are lumped together as of little direct interest as customers; whether mewling and puking or creeping unwilling to school, they are deficient in purchasing power but not to be overlooked as consumers. The first direct customer segment consists of the young independent earners, who are likely – if they have escaped the trap of juvenile unemployment – to have more money to spend on themselves than they will again till much later in life. Next come the young couples, still without children but struggling to get a home together with all the material and financial problems that this involves. Next is the harassing stage of raising a family, when budgets are still likely to be tight and expenditure directed towards necessities rather than luxuries. Then comes a second period of relative affluence – in fair round belly with expense account lunches lined – when the earning capacity of one or both partners (assuming the partnership has survived) is likely to be at its height and children have departed. Finally arrives retirement – not as impoverished for some, with mortgages paid off and insurance policies matured, as dismissive terms like OAP and group DE would imply. Like any form of segmentation, the life cycle concept is pretty crude; the single-parent family and the two-earner family at the same stage in the life cycle are poles apart in lifestyle. But in appropriate markets, it can help to concentrate the marketing planner's mind on real people living real lives.

Yet another approach to segmentation appropriate to some markets is the *ethnographic*. When there are concentrations of different ethnic groups within a market, with different cultural needs, consumption habits – especially food and drink – or languages, it can make good commercial sense to cater to these special needs. It is vital, of course, to distinguish between segmentation and segregation; but the cultivation of the black market (black in the ethnic sense) in the US has not interfered with the battle against racialism; nor has the marketing of Indian and Chinese foods or the opening of foreign banks in London to cater to the needs of national groups had much bearing either way on the absorption of those groups into the wider UK community. Indeed ethnic foods and ethnic banks have often widened their attraction to embrace a growing number of non-ethnic customers – a not uncommon manifestation of the imprecise art of market segmentation, where you aim for a precisely defined target and end up by winning a number of unexpected passers-by.

A slightly metaphysical variant on demographics is the *psychographic* approach, which requires market researchers and planners to analyse a potential market according to the psychological attributes of different customer groups; and to concentrate product development and promotional effort on a particular group with a definable psychological need that it is possible and profitable to satisfy (naturally, within the law). Under this theory catering to the urge to take drugs is inadmissible (though it has not been unknown for otherwise reputable manufacturers of quite ordinary drugs to hint in less advanced countries that their products have remarkable aphrodisiac qualities). The gambling market, on the other hand, if rather less profitable, can be legitimate if you have a good lawyer. Catering to the psychological needs of people (mostly, it seems, young women) who want to be skinnier than nature intended is equally legitimate, provided you steer well clear of food and drugs legislation. Wider in its application is the psychological tendency of some people – an undesirably small minority, from the marketing viewpoint – to be reassured by a high price. The bank manager who was once asked by his assistant manager what he should charge a particular customer for an exceptional service would probably have been insulted if anyone had called him an expert in psychographics. But his answer was eminently psychological: 'Flatter him, dear boy, with a handsome fee; he will boast about it at the chamber of commerce.'

Banking: an example of customer creation

The banking and financial services market is, in fact, an arena in which the practice of all the interactive aspects of market segmentation, from the physical to the psychological, is peculiarly necessary. For anybody but the subsistence farmer, the nomad tribesman or the penniless down-and-out (fortunately, there are relatively few of each category in the UK), money is a sensitive and personal matter. But banks, particularly the large clearing banks, have been driven to increasing depersonalization by the need to rely on the computer for coping with the much wider use of banking services since the war. Though the British banking industry came later to modern marketing than consumer products industries, market segmentation has begun to play a major role in the banks' marketing thinking.

It has been greatly assisted by improvements in cost accounting systems, making it possible to get a reasonably accurate fix on the profitability of different customer segments. This has made it possible to confirm what was previously only suspected: that the unbanked, who are expensively persuaded to open a bank account for the first time, tend to be unprofitable to the bank that wins their favours, whereas the affluent customer who deals in large numbers – whether large deposits or large overdrafts – tends to be highly profitable; and that the large multinational company may be the jewel in the bank's crown but, because of its ability to negotiate the best terms by playing off one bank against another, is likely to contribute less to even its lead bank's profits than are much more modest concerns.

One bank, relatively small on its own account but a member of a large financial services group, undertook the task – within overall group strategy – of increasing its market share of the affluent personal customer segment. It was an attractive task because of the proven profitability of this segment. But there was the inevitable catch that banks and para-banking institutions around the world had also recognized its profitability, so competition was becoming fiercer by the month; and in any market increasing competition usually leads to declining profitability. The need was clearly to create not just customers but profitable customers for the bank.

Where should they start? The bank's management refrained from the impulsive policy, adopted by other banks in the past, of voting a large advertising budget to tell the world that more customers would be welcome and letting it go at that. They couldn't afford enough money to attract the world's attention over the clamour of competitive claims; and anyway they didn't want the whole world as customers, just a modest slice of the upper crust. Instead they started by taking a long, hard look at their own strengths and weaknesses and having a long, hard think about the customer segments to whom the strengths would be more important than the weaknesses.

First came *weaknesses* – being more painful to accept, though in some cases translatable into strengths. Their *smallness* was an obvious weakness from the viewpoint of very large customers, requiring a wide range of specialist services; but others, for whom small is beautiful, might well regard it as a strength. Perhaps the feeling of smallness and intimacy could be preserved, despite an expansionist programme, by concentrating on establishing close personal relationships with customers, getting to know their needs, and subcontracting some of the specialist services required to the parent group or outside experts.

The bank had *few branches outside London or overseas.* That was a weakness that could be cured – at a cost – by planting colonies outside the metropolis. But perhaps it wasn't really a weakness in the short run, considering the limited number of new customers the bank could handle without reducing standards of service, and the relatively high proportion of rich individuals, British and foreign, who find it convenient to have a banking facility in London.

A *shortage of high-calibre, well-trained executives* was another identifiable weakness – not an uncommon one for a service business, but a threat to service quality, if the rate of expansion were to outstrip the growth of new capacity. The shortage was most marked in the area of marketing expertise; in the past a high level of technical banking expertise and a good, if not widespread, reputation had attracted enough new customers year by year to make active marketing unnecessary (though some might argue that if it had been practised earlier, the bank would still be independent rather than absorbed into a larger group).

An *inadequate management information and financial control system* was another weakness from a marketing viewpoint. You can't seriously contemplate investing in planned business development, if you lack the systems to determine which market segments or products are likely to produce the best return, or to measure the results of any new initiatives.

Last and in some ways least, because most easily cured, was the bank's amiable weakness of *hiding its light under a bushel*. Its customers recognized and appreciated the ways in which the bank differed from its competitors. But potential customers, with similar tastes and requirements, knew very little about it; and even customers were singularly ill-informed on the range of services it had to offer. This weakness in projection was not attributable simply to lack of advertising and PR; the bank itself had not a very clear image of how it was seen, and would wish to be seen, through the eyes of potential customers.

As for *strengths*, the most conspicuous was a tradition (more pretentiously describable as a corporate culture) of *good manners* stretching back over 300 years of history as a private bank and colouring the behaviour of everybody from the telephone operators and receptionists upwards. It would be an exaggeration to say that manners makyth bank; efficiency and expertise also have a certain importance. But manners certainly makyth an agreeable contrast to that exceptionally unmannerly character, the computer.

A second strength was the *existing customer base*, both personal and corporate. Having been built up over the years more by happy accident than by sociological design, with accounts handed down from father to son or daughter, and from one financial director to his successor, it was not quite as homogeneous a family as might be desired. But it was already heavily concentrated in the two segments of affluent individuals and family businesses or partnerships, which were beginning to emerge as the priority target groups; and many of them were not yet making full use of the financial services the bank could offer.

Another strength was a relatively *high staff to customer ratio*. The accountants, it is true, could stigmatize this as a weakness – proof of inefficiency and overmanning. But provided that the extra people were allocated to the improvement of customer service, it would help to establish a real difference between the bank and its competitors.

And provided that customers were willing to pay more for the improved service – which on the whole they were. A major strength of the bank was a *pricing policy*, accepted by customers, which left elbow room for the marketer's dream of a genuinely better product, whose price is evidence of its superiority.

Reviewing the bank's strengths and weaknesses took management a long way down the road towards drawing a *portrait of its target customer*, or more realistically target customer segments. Complete homogeneity would have been convenient; but it had to be recognized that within the category of affluent individual there were at least four subsegments with different needs and attitudes represented by old wealth and new wealth, each subdivided into UK resident and non-resident; and business customers were different again, though conveniently enough the same individual could be the key both to personal and to corporate business. Analysis of the practical lessons learned by the bank's directors and managers in dealing with individual customers in the target segments and of account histories, reinforced by independent customer attitude and behaviour research, helped to construct recognizable identikit portraits of the customers the bank already had and those it would like to have.

So what did the bank need to do to create new or improved relationships with the target customer as portrayed? Management identified a list of interconnected areas which needed to be progressively strengthened, if the dream of more beautiful relationships was to become reality. Inevitably, in a service business, *people* came top of the list. There was a nucleus of the right people with the right skills and attitudes; but there were not enough of them to handle the rate of business growth that was envisaged. The management development plan needed to be reviewed, specialists recruited and job-related training stepped up. If people were to improve their performance and all advance in the right direction, questions of motivation and internal communications had to be reconsidered.

Products came next on the list. In banking genuinely innovative products are rare, and when invented soon imitated. Being small, the bank lacked the resources for major innovations; and in any case its chosen difference lay in its style and level of service rather than radically different products. All the same, there was ample room to modify standard products so that they fitted the needs of target customer segments better; and to package them more attractively and conveniently from the customer's viewpoint. This raised practical questions, such as who should be responsible for product improvement and development, how should new ideas be fed in and progressively refined or rejected, how should production and marketing considerations be reconciled, and what provisions should be made for test marketing major new developments. Somewhat painfully, mainly because of people's reluctance to change existing habits, new procedures were hammered out.

Premises were another factor to consider. For the immediate future there was enough additional business to be had in London, without the need to invest in provincial or overseas offices. But some time in the future they would be needed, and would need to be manned. Better start thinking now about their location, size and character (full-scale branches, representative offices, or something new and different using modern technology?) and about the manpower implications.

All of this raised more fundamental questions of *organizational structure*. A new marketing services department had been grafted on when the decision to expedite growth was first reached. It made a contribution but, lacking executive authority, suffered all the frustrations and indignities of Machiavelli's advocate of change. Something more dynamic had to be considered. Would it put too many noses out of joint if the long-term banking convention of the manager as salesman were abandoned and the business development and customer relations function separated organizationally from the managerial function?

Taking action on these different fronts and combining them into a phased plan, complete with deadlines and targets, into which it was not too difficult to feed a promotional plan, naturally took time – the better part of two years, in fact. But business as usual had to be maintained during alterations; and it was rightly felt that, despite all frustrations, it was better to cajole people than to bully them into accepting change. Now the grand plan is beginning to move into action. First results are promising. By the year 2000 or even sooner, we should know for certain whether they got it right.

A recipe for customer creation

Recipes are as stultifying in customer creation as they are in cookery; it is creative imagination, making the very best of available ingredients, that differentiates the masterpiece from the mundane in both cases. But there are some standard ingredients that are essential, like a basic béchamel, to a wide range of customer creative dishes. Seven are particularly important:

1 Remember that whether you have one customer or a million you are always in the end striking a bargain. So find out what the customer really wants and give him or her – as well as yourself – a fair deal.

2 It's easier to understand and satisfy one customer than a million. To have literally only one customer, though not unknown, is generally imprudent. But whether the scale of your business requires 100 customers or 10 million, you should try to come as close as possible to the single-customer situation by slicing the mass into homogeneous segments with similar needs and attitudes.

3 Paint a portrait of your composite customer or customers, using a combination of first-hand impressions and independent research. See that it is metaphorically pinned up not just in your own caravan – like Montgomery's picture of Rommel – but above the workplace of everybody in the company.

4 Make everybody understand that a bargain involves more than superlative salesmanship and deafening promotion; it's a two-

way relationship, involving product, price, delivery, after-sales service and style on one side, and satisfaction, tell-your-friends and come-back-for-more on the other.

5 If either side has to make adjustments to preserve the relationship, it had better be you. You need the customer more than the customer needs you.

6 When you've got something to shout about, shout. When you haven't, save your breath and your money.

7 For 'customer' read *profitable customer* throughout. Unprofitable customers should be made profitable or shed; why should the profitable subsidize them?

5 Tying up the loose ends

Many years ago, when I was still a trifle naïve (perhaps I still am), I found myself addressing a gathering of Industrial Society members. I held forth with youthful enthusiasm about the role of the marketing manager and the product manager in planning and co-ordinating the forward thrust of an organization.

At the end of my oration, I rather smugly invited questions. 'I'm a little puzzled', said a grizzled gentleman in the third row. 'If all that is what the marketing manager does, what in the world does the managing director do?' 'Good question,' said I, blushing and playing for time, 'and what is your job?' 'Oh, I'm the managing director of Thingummy & Co.'

I'm still exercising my *esprit de l'escalier* (a long, long staircase) to elaborate the urbane and witty answer I should have made in place of my lame apologia. I suppose I could have pontificated about management being a team effort, like cabinet government, with the managing director playing the prime minister's role of *primus* (or *prima*) *inter pares*; about the need for co-ordinating groups, where the activity of one department impinges upon others; and about the logic of having these groups headed by the individual (by definition a marketing man) most closely in touch with the customer, who in the end has life-or-death powers over the organization. But this would have begged many questions, including the obvious fact that some prime ministers are conspicuously more prime than others, and that some managing directors prefer to be their own marketing directors, relegating the marketing manager to the role of technical assistant.

The product manager concept

Nevertheless the concept of the product manager (also known as brand manager, project manager or marketing manager) as coordinator of all the organization's activities affecting its relationship with a defined group of customers is perhaps the most valuable of the marketing theories that have developed since the war. It recognizes the fact that satisfied customers are the end product not just of slick advertising and appealing presentation, but of the product's ability to meet their functional and emotional needs, an acceptable price, efficient delivery, after-sales service and good personal relations between customers and those of the organization's employees that they meet face to face, by telephone or through correspondence. In an ideal world all of these elements would be optimized by the relevant functional manager. But in practice the organization needs either to earn a profit or at least to stay within an agreed budget – which means that there have to be adjustments here and concessions there in order to balance the books. Somebody has to negotiate maybe with the production manager in order to convince him that some of the costly product refinements which delight his technological soul are not sufficiently important to the customer to justify a higher price; or with the sales manager to persuade him that higher sales must be achieved, perhaps by opening up new channels of distribution, perhaps by special deals and offers, in order to reduce unit costs; or with the financial controller to persuade him that accepting lower margins in the short run will extend the product's life and produce higher profits in the long run; or maybe to persuade the personnel manager that better training of staff in customer relations will pay dividends in measurable revenue terms.

The concept also recognizes the inherent contradiction between the belief, founded on practical experience of the limitations of human comprehension and managerial skills, that small is beautiful, and the tendency of mammoth international organizations to grow even larger by swallowing others scarcely smaller than themselves. It is difficult for the chief executive of Megalopolitan Enterprises International, perpetually in conference with his bankers about the latest takeover to be plotted or evaded, to empathize with his unknown hordes of customers. The product manager concept, allied to the concept of market segmentation, can do a lot to lessen the force of the contradiction. It is flexible enough to be extended from its original sense of managing the relationship between a specific product and the customers who buy it (or might be persuaded to buy it) to managing the organization's relationship with a defined segment of its customers, covering the full range of products purchased by them. And it can be particularly valuable in the case of new products or projects, when an idea has to be turned into a business (or written off as unworkable, as the case may be).

But need the product or project manager be a card-carrying marketing man and a member of the marketing department? Logically the answer is no. He can just as well be – and has been known to be – an accountant, a technician or a general manager. Indeed it is possible to dream of a day when all managers are first and foremost marketing men, accepting rather than simply paying lip service to the old saw that 'The customer is king'; and marketing managers who fail to recognize the interdependence of the total organization are relegated to the role of research, advertising or sales technicians.

However, dealing with people and the facts of corporate life as they are today, there is a strong argument for accepting the marketing department as the normal repository for the product management function. This is the fact that a marketing department with a soundly based information system has one trump card to play in the interdepartmental disputes which inevitably occur in the development of any commercial project; it knows what is going on in the marketplace and it can predict (not always accurately, but more reliably than internally oriented departments) the commercial outcome of alternative courses of action. To bring Francis Bacon up to date, '*market* knowledge itself is power.'

Just as well for the exposed product manager, nominally responsible for the profitability of the product or customer segment assigned to him, who has precious little power apart from market knowledge. His apple cart can always be upset not only by the knavish tricks of competitors or unpredictable shifts in market conditions, but by the actions of colleagues, well-intentioned from their own viewpoint, over which he has no control other than his persuasive tongue. If the sales manager decides to give a lower priority to his product or the production manager to reduce the stock cover, both in the interest of greater efficiency, there is little he can do about it except to exercise the right of appeal, which he may or may not have, to the chief executive.

The accounts department's ability to reduce or increase reported profits by a stroke of the pen can be particularly galling, as the misadventures of the product manager described in Chapter 2 demonstrated. The 'bottom line' is not the be-all and end-all of marketing, which should comprehend wider considerations such as customer satisfaction, social acceptability and the long-term future. But it tends to be the main criterion by which executive performance is measured and remuneration determined. So it is not enough for a product manager to be an expert in market research, communications, sales organization and planning. He must also understand the mysteries and minefields of finance, including the particular accountancy conventions used to measure profitability in his own organization; if he has a best friend in the accounts department, so much the better.

Understanding the products or services he sets out to market at least as well as the customer, and the interaction between production and marketing, is equally important. The tradition in Clarks of Street that every management trainee should make himself a pair of shoes early in his career was perhaps overdoing it; the outcome was some of the most expensive and uncomfortable shoes ever known. But the principle was sound. It was learned by experience (a far more effective way of learning, alas, than books like this) by a team of marketing refugees from a leading washing powder company who took over the management of a firm that manufactured washing machines. Not exactly a leap into the unknown, you might think. Not so. In the washing powder company efficient production and physical distribution could be taken for granted; sales fluctuations could be looked after with relative ease by running the soap tower a few hours more or a few hours less that week. The difference between profit and loss lay in the marketing and sales departments' ability to maintain market share and maximize the margin between standard product costs and net sales value. The production cost of the washing machines in contrast was extremely sensitive both to fluctuations in sales volume and to modifications in product features. The difference between profit and loss lay less in the traditional area of marketing and sales than in adhering to the most economical production schedules and only demanding product modifications when there was irrefutable evidence that the cost could be recovered in additional sales or higher prices. The marketing men had to unlearn their marketing dogma that the customer is always right in favour of a modified version, 'He's right, if he's prepared to pay'; and to spend as much time in colloquy with factory management as in organizing consumer research and chatting up the trade.

But of course the need for the marketing manager or brand manager in his co-ordinating role to understand the other management disciplines does not absolve him from his primary role of championing the customer's cause within the organization. The archetypal complaint, 'What a wonderful airline (or camel train) we could run, if it weren't for the passengers' does afflict almost all administrators and technicians, particularly when they rise to positions of power remote from the need to do simple deals with simple people. Prime ministers need to be reminded that they owe their eminence to the suffrage of simple cits, and will lose the next election if they forget it. Bankers need to be reminded that all their money (actually other people's money) will be useless unless they offer their customers a fair deal. Inventors need to be reminded that their brain children will never get off the drawing board unless some customers are convinced that there's something in it for them. The marketing manager's first responsibility, once he has done his market research, assembled all his facts and figures and tied up the loose ends, is to do the persuading.

Where does product responsibility end?

The more colourful writers about management often describe the product manager as product champion, dramatizing his responsibility to fight and die for the product's or project's success, rather than simply recording its rise and (all too often) fall; they also emphasize the need for a senior management godfather – a slightly less chivalric title – to guide him through the maze of corporate politics. How far in practice can he go in co-ordinating all the factors that underpin success, without incurring the implacable wrath of every senior manager in sight?

Much depends on the culture of the organization concerned, whether it is obstinately hierarchical, like most large banks, in which any departure from the rulebook is frowned on (often for good reason, since other people's money is at stake), or makes a fetish, like 3M, of encouraging enterprise down the line and accepting failure as long as it is not habitual. But let us trace the history of a composite bright young man, constantly learning from experience as a brand manager within the contemporary concept of the term from 1950 till 1980 – somewhat cynical by then, but still learning.

In the 1950s James Doughty worked for the British subsidiary of an American processed food company that had a good reputation as a training ground for marketing management (before the business schools got going in this country, ambitious marketing men were well advised to attend Heinz College or the University of P & G). Thoroughly indoctrinated in the marketing unities – the right product at the right place at the right price and the right time – Doughty was entrusted as new product brand manager with the UK branch of one of the company's moderately successful American brands.

He followed the rulebook meticulously. He carried out market research to establish the existence of a market gap – or at least the absence of a serious direct competitor. He organized taste tests to establish consumer acceptability, and arranged for the American flavour to be modified to suit the British palate. He employed design consultants to develop and test a brand name and packaging, and appointed a hotshot advertising agency to go through the orthodox procedures of motivational research and copytesting leading to integrated consumer and trade campaigns, first in a test market and then nationally.

But when it came to the crunch, the launch was a shambles. The advertising won universal praise from the advertising profession, but exasperated both the consuming public and the grocery trade because the new wonder product was simply not available in the shops. The factory had been unexpectedly late in its delivery dates (it was blamed on late delivery of the packaging material) and the product had taken unexpectedly long (in marketing the unexpected must always be expected) to get out of wholesale and multiple warehouses on to the shelves. By the time it was widely displayed, the initial burst of advertising was finished, everybody had lost interest and there was little movement from shelf to shopping bag. Moreover, as the company accountants belatedly pointed out, even if test market sales targets had been achieved, the weight of advertising there could never have been reproduced nationally and left any room for profit.

Doughty, being a thoroughly doughty individual, survived the débâcle. He learnt from it that nobody's promises could be accepted at their face value; so constant checking and niggling was needed with all the internal departments, the external suppliers and the distributors, any of whom can torpedo an otherwise hopeful project. He was also largely responsible for his company's decision to supplement its sales force with a merchandising force, with the never-ending task of building supermarket displays for the company's products (and occasionally, through some unfortunate mischance, upsetting the displays of competitive products). But by 1960 he had been headhunted on behalf of a British packaged goods company, which hoped to use his midatlantic expertise in furthering its declared resolve to become more marketing oriented.

Here he found a rather different situation. By this time the technique of market segmentation had begun to be widely accepted, which was just as well for his new employers. Doughty had learned enough from his previous misadventures to resist the pressure for instant miracles and to spend some time sizing up the situation. The consumer research that he commissioned (none had been done before his arrival) confirmed what he had suspected from looking at the company's products and their pricing – that their appeal was largely confined to a relatively narrow segment of the population, unlike the mass market appeal to which he had previously grown accustomed. Trade research showed that distribution was distinctly patchy, with concentrations of strength mostly in the more old-fashioned outlets and the more conservative parts of the country. Since the funds available for advertising and sales promotion were quite modest, there was no escaping a segmented marketing strategy, concentrating effort and expenditure on reinforcing the strong points. By dint of this strategy and working with his colleagues to improve the co-ordination of the company's limited resources – adjusting the deployment of the sales force and the delivery system on a more selective basis – Doughty managed to improve profitability and extend the company's lease of life. His colleagues came to admit that, while marketing was not the miracle worker they had hoped for, the marketing approach had some practical merit.

What James Doughty had failed to reckon with was the fact that the company's basic cost structure was uncompetitive. The ratios of production costs, selling costs, distribution costs and administrative costs to sales were all too high, none of them by very much but cumulatively to a degree that made it impossible to offer the consumer real value for money. Doughty's relationships with his colleagues and with his managing director were good enough to ensure co-operation as long as it was relatively painless; but they did not stretch far enough to carry the day when it came to truly painful belt-tightening in individual departments. Eventually the inevitable happened and a takeover substituted throat-cutting for belt-tightening.

Doughty, falling on his feet as usual, moved onwards and financially (if not hierarchically) upwards to a marketing management position in one of the clearing banks, which had taken a belated fancy in the 1970s to marketing (whatever that might be). Here at least there should be no problem of straitened finances. Nor was there. His new masters, being used to dealing in billions, were not dismayed by the notion of spending many millions on promotion; and being rather naïve about marketing, were not as fussy about the return on their promotional investment as on more habitual forms of investment.

But there were other problems, arising principally from the fact that bank marketing in the early days was a rather lowly staff function, separate from the line management structure which had its main contract with customers at branch level and wended its way upward through area offices and regional offices to the top managerial stratosphere, whose inhabitants – before they became supermen – had spent their formative years as branch managers. At all levels the prevailing culture was founded on what from the banks' viewpoint was prudent lending, but from the customers' viewpoint looked like a system for raking in the public's money in good times and refusing to part with it in times of need.

Doughty had comparatively little difficulty in improving the bank's standards of marketing communication both through media advertising and through brochures and other printed material; it was mainly a matter of convincing his bosses that you had to talk to people in language they understood, even if this involved some abandonment of bankerly dignity (he found, slightly to his surprise, that most bankers are actually human beings). He was also able to develop some new products – most of them actually old products polished up and repackaged. But none of his projects was as successful as it might have been, because he was unable to secure the personal commitment at all levels which is essential in what is still – despite computers, cash dispensers and other hardware – a personal service business. When he left the bank, his successor inherited a better prospect than Doughty had found, partly because pressure of competition in the financial services industry had accelerated acceptance of marketing principles, and partly because he had devoted almost as much time and effort to 'selling' marketing internally as he had to marketing the bank's products. But only here and there was it possible to mount fully co-ordinated marketing projects.

Doughty left, in fact, in 1980 to set up his own business making and marketing training films and videos. As marketing manager, sales manager, production manager and finance manager, he finds for the first time in his life that he has no problem with internal communications. His marketing manager and sales manager (both himself) have no problem communicating while shaving in the morning, or even through an active subconscious while asleep at night. His production manager (himself), looking forward to marketing his output, fully recognizes the need to put customer benefit ahead of artistic self-expression. His finance manager (himself again), having mortgaged the family home to raise capital, is fully alive to the importance of a positive cash flow.

The only trouble is that the business has now taken off and is rapidly growing. Soon he must delegate some of his responsibilities. What will he let go?

6 Coming to terms with the computer

'Used in conjunction with the Modaptor, the Qcode terminal emulator is compatible with most modems on the market.' Why, yes, of course. Every schoolboy (and schoolgirl) knows what *that* means. The trouble is that many of the managers who are running businesses today left school in the old-fashioned days when it was not customary to learn computer language before you learnt to spell. They are apt to ask, carefully concealing their non-comprehension, 'But what do I do with the damn thing?'

Computers are *potentially* a boon and a blessing to the marketing manager – or the marketing-minded general manager – seeking to plan and control the development of a total business or of some project within the totality. Their ability to store, process and regurgitate information can be immensely valuable in facilitating the marketing task of bringing together relevant data from a variety of sources fast enough to help improve the quality of managerial decision-making. Their use in the construction of market models into which assumptions about change, whether voluntary or involuntary, can be injected is equally valuable in facilitating the marketing task of predicting the consequences of innovative actions, and of providing an early warning system of threats arising from competitors' innovations or from changes in the environment. Their ability to collate and summarize at great speed internal data about sales, costs, stock levels and profit margins make it far easier to discharge the marketing obligation to monitor the results of any initiatives and take appropriate action when things are not going according to plan.

But so far marketing and the computer, more or less con-temporaries in their arrival on the business scene, have failed most lamentably to come to terms. The full potential of an immensely powerful instrument has yet to be realized by the great majority of marketing departments. What can be a very useful servant, if properly mastered, can become a menace if a proliferation of figures is accepted as a substitute for thinking.

The problem of communication

The first problem is one of communication – computer boffin and marketing boffin bombarding each other with broadsides of jargon across a great divide of non-comprehension. Often there is an element of one-upmanship in this; if people cannot understand what you are talking about, it must surely prove that you are an expert. Communications are improving, now that data processing specialists have added the new adjective 'user-friendly' to their vocabulary, and marketing men have come to understand the benefits and limitations of computers. Computers themselves are learning to communicate in plain English (or German or Japanese) instead of requiring the services of an interpreter.

No longer is it likely that marketing managers will suffer the fate of one I knew years ago, who finally responded to repeated requests from the relatively enlightened EDP consultants who were installing his company's new central computer system that he specify his requirements for sales targeting and control purposes. 'Wouldn't it be nice to know, for example a couple of days after the end of each month, the sales performance of each area salesman?' 'Why yes, of course.' 'And presumably the figures should be broken down by product?' 'Yes, indeed.' 'And by type of outlet?' 'That would be useful.' 'And there should be year ago comparisons, and comparisons against target?' 'Of course.' 'Then, naturally, you'll want both gross and net sales figures, allowing for discounts and so on.' 'If you say so.'

At this point he thought no more about it until several months later, when the first monthly printouts arrived on his desk, completely covering it and overflowing on to adjacent surfaces. It was an appalling sight; his immediate response was to catch the first train to London for an emergency session with the advertising agency. They at least would listen respectfully to his animadversions on the corporate campaign and refrain from burying him under mountains of paper.

On the train home (having been satisfactorily beastly to the agency) he reflected that perhaps there was a lesson to be learned from the cryptic sign '*Think*' that IBM handed out to all and sundry in its early days. Think, perhaps about what information you need from the computer, what form you need it in, and how you and your staff are going to handle it when you get it. Otherwise the computer, a mindless though infinitely powerful Pygmalion that does exactly what it's told, however daft, is bound to overwhelm you.

Accountants in the driving seat

Part of the trouble for marketers is that computer installations have not yet recovered from their early bias towards accountancy applications. Computers were originally sold to accountants, often by accountants, on the claim that they would reduce the cost of keeping company and customer accounts, payrolls, invoicing, stock records and so on. In the event they seldom actually reduced costs, though in many expanding firms and industries such as banking they prevented what would otherwise have been an unaffordable explosion in demand for clerical labour (creating employment is all very well, but the mind boggles at the thought of all those bored bookkeepers posting all those innumerable ledgers). What they did do, almost inadvertently because management outside the accounts department was not all that interested, was to make much more readily and rapidly accessible a wealth of information about the company's current and past performance that could be exceedingly useful for planning and control purposes – provided that the relevant managers were organized and mentally equipped to use it.

Marketing managers have been as much to blame as general managers in this respect. The banking industry, where mainframe computers were first installed to handle customer accounts and the interbank clearing system, was conspicuous in its initial failure to harness computer power for the purpose of planned business development. It was customary, though dismaying, for advisers on bank marketing in the mid 1960s to get the answer to innocent questions about how many customers they had:

'Well, we don't exactly know.'

'But can't you organize a special computer run and let me know in the morning?'

'That wouldn't help. You see the computer is programmed to handle customer accounts, not customers. It knows very little about the customers behind the accounts, or how many accounts the average customer has with us.'

'So what do you do if you want to promote a service that is likely to be of interest to certain types of customer but not to others, and need to know how many customers you have in that category?'

'We can arrange a hand count from branch records. But this is expensive and time consuming, so we can only do it on a sample basis; and in any case branch records are not what they were before customers' accounts were transferred to the central computer. Or, of course, we and our competitors – who are all in the same boat as we are – can obtain approximate figures from the syndicated market research carried out for the industry, also naturally on a sample basis. But we are promised that the new model computer system that is being worked on will tell us what we need to know about our customers, including the relative profitability of different categories.'

'How soon?'

'Ten years, with any luck.'

The poor service offered by the banks' computer systems to their marketing departments should not have come as such a shock in the 1960s, because of the lowly status of bank marketing in those days. Marketing was generally regarded by the banks as a rather irritating side issue, an activity that should be confined to non-essentials like advertising, and not allowed to interfere with the way the business was run. By now the top brass in the clearing and other banks talk familiarly of marketing strategy, market segmentation, product development and the like. It is widely accepted that effective marketing cannot be a painless, hands-off activity, but must involve all of line management in a variety of combined operations. Yet the typical computer dialogue of the 1960s could still take place in most large British banks in the mid 1980s – except that the vital improvements are a realistic year or two away, rather than a pie-in-the-sky ten years.

The menace of GIGO

A great hazard of the computer, for those unfamiliar with its funny ways, is its reputation for infallibility. Attaching the adjective 'computerized' to almost any set of figures about the present, the future or the past somehow makes it seem more authentic. It is true enough that computers do their sums more accurately as well as far faster than any human being. But they are also more exposed to the GIGO – garbage in, garbage out – factor; where a human being will stop and say 'Hey, that doesn't make sense' to an anomalous figure, computers are generally uncritical and will swallow obediently all the data and instructions that are fed to them. It was not just old-fashioned prejudice, I fancy, that made the financial head of a large insurance company confess to me that he had always been uneasy about their quarterly results since the transfer from a manual to a computerized system. 'In the old days it was three weeks of agony, but at least I was on top of every step in the process and could pick up mistakes as they happened. Now it's all over in three days, and I'm never quite sure that some ghastly error hasn't flashed by undetected.'

Notoriously the favourite time for GIGO to pounce is during the process of transferring some procedure from a manual or old computer system to a new one. A famous instance of this in the annals of marketing occasioned the downfall of a marketing expert, better known for his innovative and expansionist skills than for any great interest in the flip side of marketing – counting the cost of his actions.

The origin of this disaster, now long in the past, was a keen awareness of the opportunities for increased control, enhanced knowledge, improved customer service and real savings that a computerized accounting and invoicing system can offer the marketing department. You know what's happening faster; you can make quick analyses to identify the types of outlet, district, salesman or product responsible for some disturbance in the planned course of events; you can help your customers by giving them more detailed analyses of their transactions with you; and by speedier invoicing you can reduce the cost of financing your receivables.

That is, if the computer gets it right. In this case it didn't get it even nearly right. When the button was pressed on the new system – rather early on, because our anti-hero had a reputation for dynamic action to sustain – the customers received a barrage of invoices that a large proportion of them rejected as inaccurate. An acrimonious correspondence would have been bad enough, but worse was to follow. It appeared that in the transfer to the new electronic system, the old manual records had been destroyed, leaving no leg for the company to stand on. The final outcome, coincidental with the ceremony of the golden handshake, was a circular letter to tens of thousands of customers, saying in effect, 'All right then, you tell us how much you owe us.' So they did, after a fashion.

The fact that the human attendants of the computer can err should not of course be held against the sacred monster itself. It really is invaluable, when properly used. But if fed inaccurate data or badly programmed it can mislead on a more massive scale than mere mortals. A healthy scepticism is in order.

The computerized crystal ball

In the early post-war years the task of forecasting sales performance and market share was not a great problem for most marketing managers; quite simply they didn't have to do it. Sales were determined by raw material availability and production capacity, and the marketing department would be informed by higher authority what next year's budget – it always seemed to be 10 per cent up on last year – should be. Well within living memory, the main task of the salesmen representing a market leader like Heinz (hundreds of them, slogging around on foot) was to inform their grateful customers in the grocery trade what this month's allocation of the 57 varieties would be; their efforts, such as they were, were supported by an exceedingly modest advertising campaign, proclaiming that 'Back they come, one by one.'

As the balance of market power shifted, at different rates in different markets, the tradition of an imposed 10 per cent up on last year lingered on, motivated now less by production capacity than by the finance department's appreciation of what the stock market was looking for. The advent of the computer as an aid to better forecasting should have improved the situation. Realistic forecasting models would have brought out the fact that performance in a marketplace unrestricted by shortages or cartels was determined at least as much by customers, competitors and the general economic change as by the efforts of the individual company, however large.

Unhappily the computer's enormous facility for doing sums, plus its control as a rule by the finance department, encouraged the engrained habit of relying almost entirely on the projection of trends for sales and profit forecasting; forecasts would be much more elaborate, but the end product tended to be the same as before – 10 per cent up on last year.

So here was another area where the computer, a potential friend of marketing, could have a hostile effect by encouraging a mindless and mechanistic approach. It is possible certainly that, if not blinded with science, managers would have been no readier to listen to the people actually in touch with customers; and no better at foreseeing the major discontinuities, like the shift from shortage to glut of consumer products in the 1960s, and the escalation of energy costs in the 1970s. But it is tempting to believe that, in the former case at least, the more extroverted approach and the willingness to think through the consequences of observable events that market-ing is supposed to encourage would have brought about faster reactions – if only human thought and discussion had not been drowned in computer printouts.

It's a sexy form of investment

One of the most sacred of all the establishment's sacred cows is that the future of the UK economy is bound up with higher investment in information technology – the big IT that combines computers with electronic communications. This implies, presumably, that British industry should invest more both in the production and in the application of such systems.

Well, perhaps. It is certainly galling that we should have an adverse balance of payments in an area where so much of the primary invention, from Turing the father of modern computers onwards, originated in this country. But the sexiness of phrases like 'innovative technology' and 'modern science' should not prevent the down-to-earth marketing man from asking his eternal question, 'Where's the benefit?' It flatters the ego to have the most up-to-date electronic office or the most powerful computer system in town; but it's only justified commercially if it enables you to serve the group of customers on whom your business depends. But what happens to the national balance of payments if we buy all our chips from Osaka instead of producing them in Pontypool? That, it could be answered, is the whole point of international trade. You concentrate on doing better what you are already best at doing, and buy in what others do better. If you are better at producing potato chips than silicon chips, don't diversify from the former to the latter, but buy in the silicon chips you need to make still better and cheaper potato chips.

The information overload

The marketer's task of collecting information about customers, competitors, economic conditions and the market at large is another field where the computer misused can be a false friend. The wide availability of data banks, whose terminals will tell you all you need to know (and a lot you don't need to know) about almost everything, is a temptation to commit the cardinal sin of all market researchers and other information gatherers – to accumulate information for its own sake and not as a means to a practical, profitable end. So is the facility for a marketing services or market intelligence department to build up its own computerized data base (far more capacious than any old-fashioned filing system), happy in the belief that it is creating a store of wealth for the organization. True enough, if it enables the department to answer the questions asked by the organization's decision-makers and action men more speedily and comprehensively than in the past. But untrue if the questions are never asked; for, unlike wine, information does not improve with age. The value of a large supply of ready answers depends on correct anticipation of the questions that will be asked – and perhaps on some discreet lobbying to make sure that the anticipated questions are actually asked and acted on.

This may read like a very curmudgeonly, even Luddite chapter. Why look an extremely powerful gift horse in the mouth? The computer, after all, can greatly extend the reach and the analytical capacity of marketing management. Perhaps the managers who have been disappointed by the computer's contribution were simply reflecting the age-old nostalgia for their youthful days when life was simpler, they had fewer customers, and they knew them all personally instead of having to deal with them through an increasingly impersonal hierarchy of subordinates – aided and abetted by an even more impersonal computer system. Perhaps the yearning for simplicity is part of it, even though a well-planned computer system can actually simplify life at the top. But a more down-to-earth consideration is that even gift horses are expensive to feed and groom. Before taking on the cost of maintaining as well as buying a computer installation for marketing purposes, it is as well to be absolutely clear how it will be used and how it will earn its keep. To quote IBM again, '*Think*.'

7 I'm so busy, I've no time to think

The last chapter ended, advisedly, with the word 'think'. For failure to think clearly about all the implications of a business initiative and to think ahead about its likely consequences has been the greatest single cause of marketing's disappointing performance over the past thirty years.

It can sound pretentious to suggest that the marketing department is the main focus of constructive long-term thinking in an organization; or that bad marketing is partly to blame for the failure of the top management of the United Kingdom PLC to think through the aftermath of the Falklands adventure ('All right, with a bit of luck we win the war. But what do we do next?'), just as it is for the failure of half the small businesses started in this country to survive for more than a couple of years. But the marketing principles of finding out and thinking about the relevant facts, considering alternative courses of action arising from them, thinking imaginatively about the reactions of colleagues, customers and competitors and how they can be induced to be reasonable and see it your way, planning long term rather than short term – all of these have much wider applications than their effect on the profitability of strictly commercial concerns. And of course the marketing department – if there is a marketing department – certainly does not have the monopoly of this kind of thinking; indeed if it does not permeate the organization, the marketing department or whoever fills the marketing role will not be very effective. But the marketing department or its equivalent should play a leading part, ideally under the wing of the chief executive, in fostering the organization's thinking activities; it is well placed to do so, when it incorporates a strong market information unit, because it is in closer touch than more introverted departments with what is going on in the outside world, and more actively involved in the attempt to build durable bridges between its own essentially conservative organization ('Why do we have to change everything when it's at last beginning to run smoothly?') and the uncontrollable environment that so perversely insists on changing?

Thinking in context

But what do you mean by thinking? Is it true that organizations are generally bad at it, and if so why? A good question, though I ask it myself. I'm not talking about the kind of contemplative thinking embodied in the traditional boast: 'Sometimes I sits and thinks, and sometimes I just sits.' That is not to be despised. It can be a pleasure in itself and sometimes results in a flash of inspiration – like the answer to a knotty problem that struck Archimedes in his bathtub and sent him naked through the streets of Syracuse shouting *Eureka!*, hotly pursued (according to the cartoonist) by Mrs A., crying 'Archie, you've flooded the bathroom floor again.' Agreeable as it is, this kind of thinking has to be eschewed (except perhaps in his own bathroom) by the marketing man with an urge for survival, in favour of more action-oriented thinking processes. It is the absence of this second kind of thinking that has resulted in the cession of much of the UK domestic appliance market to the Italians and the Germans and of the television and motorcar market to the Japanese; and has allowed millions of pounds of taxpayers' money to be invested in making products like De Lorean cars that never had the remotest chance of selling in sufficient numbers.

These it might be argued are failures more of general management judgement than of specifically marketing thinking, though a larger element of marketing philosophy in the general managerial mind might have helped to avoid this. More specific to marketing is the thinking that should accompany the transition from plain, old-fashioned selling to marketing. It was exemplified at its simplest by Jim, one of the nicest and most enthusiastic sales managers I ever met. Jim's company, a manufacturer of packaged grocery products, was struggling to survive one of the more fatal commercial diseases – an absence of cost accounting controls resulting in products being sold for less than they cost to make, pack and distribute. Straightforward accountancy calculations of the ideal selling price were obviously impractical in a competitive market where the large multiples had greater bargaining power than medium-sized manufacturers; so Jim was given floor prices down to which he could negotiate with the biggest customers without actually making a loss. Jim was constantly returning to base, flushed with some new triumph.

'I've persuaded Tesco to take a first order of Bloggo.'
'That's great, Jim. What price?'
'Well, I had to shade it a bit to get in.'
'Yes, Jim, what price?'
'Well, actually. . . .'
'But Jim, *think*. Where does it get us, selling at a loss? And when did you last get a multiple buyer to pay more for a repeat delivery than for the first order?'

In the end a desperate management let Jim go – probably unwisely. He was a good salesman; and while marketing thinking about profitability and long-term consequences is fine, somebody still has to go out and make the sale.

More often the necessary thinking is rather more complex, involving the co-ordinating role of the product manager, who must continue to think simultaneously about both ends and means, particularly:

1 The role of the project for which he is responsible in the totality of corporate strategy (assuming that he is fortunate enough to obtain a clear statement of this).
2 Who the prospective customers are and what are their thoughts, needs and prejudices.
3 What benefit he can offer them and how he can best communicate this to them.
4 What price he can reasonably ask and what margin this will leave him for marketing costs and profit.
5 Whether he can widen the margin by persuading (and helping) the producer side of the organization to reduce costs, by longer runs, modifications of the product or service offered, improved delivery systems, better stock control and so on.
6 How he can best ensure the co-operation of sales people, distributors and other sections of the organization involved in the project.

7 Whether the organization has the resources to support success, as well as absorbing failure.
8 How competitors will react.
9 What is likely to go wrong and how it can be dealt with.
10 What the next step is, and the next and the next.

All of this and more must be considered, in the context not of the idealized situation of marketing theory, but in the context of the particular organization, its particular customers, its particular competitors – and the particularly obstructive personalities that have to be dealt with in any real life situation.

The enemies of thinking

The greatest enemy of the kind of long-term, comprehensive thinking that marketing at its best implies is the British – but not exclusively British – disease of *short-termitis*. It is exemplified in government by Harold Wilson's notorious remark that 'A week in politics is a long time', reflecting the unavoidable fact that for a politician, practising the art of survival, next week's parliamentary question or next year's election must loom larger than the state of the nation ten years ahead. So national assets are sold off, the next generation's income is mortgaged, fundamental issues are fudged for the sake of immediate opinion poll ratings. Similar short-term pressures affect the chief executives of businesses. If the next quarterly or half-yearly results do not satisfy the expectations of the financial analysts, some predator will pounce with a takeover bid, or the institutional investors will demand the chief executive's head on a platter. In either event Keynes's observation that 'In the long run we are all dead' has to be modified; the chief executive is dead in the short run – no encouragement at all to undertake major new projects that will pay off in five years, but depress profits in the meantime.

A congenital distaste for serious planning is another factor in short-termitis. 'You can never rely on forecasts, so why bother to plan for the unpredictable?' 'Remember George Brown's national plan.' 'Our British talent is for improvization, we always lose every battle but the last.' Yes, of course, forecasting is difficult, but a better guide into a murky future, particularly if possibilities as well as probabilities are foreseen, than staggering blindly from crisis to crisis. Yes, perhaps, we are great survivors, though one day if we persist in not thinking ahead we are going to lose the last battle too. Difficulties and half-truths are no excuse for refusal to plan for the future or (a more frequent phenomenon in large companies) to have an elaborate planning system for show rather than for use and to take major decisions not on a planned basis but on the inspiration of the moment. If you are running a one-man business you can afford to say, as I did in my salad days, 'Corporate plan? That means the mood I'm in this morning.' It is an irresponsible mode of operation for those who have the working lives of others in their hands.

The self-image of the *man of action*, prevalent in all types of organization except the academic, is a second enemy of thinking. The overflowing in-tray, the telephone calls interrupting every serious discussion, the crowded appointments book, the lament that 'I'm so busy I've no time to think', are manifestations that no observer of managerial behaviour can have escaped. It is contagious and very difficult to resist. If your boss is busy all the time, even though the results of all his activities may be unremarkable, and if one of those activities is to write the performance appraisal report on which your own promotion may depend, it can be imprudent not to follow his example. You may do the organization more good by a constructive discussion with your colleagues or by staring out of the window for half an hour and hitting on a constructive thought than by many hours of frenetic, unthinking activity; but unless the organization has been conditioned (most unusually) to respect thinkers, it will do your career no good to be identified as a bright but idle type.

Another enemy of thinking can be labelled rather pompously as the corporate culture or the not-invented-here syndrome or more simply as the *force of habit*. When an organization has become very efficient at doing whatever it does, the original or progressive thinker with a questioning mind who asks whether there's a better way to do it, or even whether it's the right thing to do in tomorrow's conditions, is unlikely to be popular; the penalty for questioning the received wisdom of the day is likely to be disparagement at best or expulsion at worst – as both the wets in the Conservative party and the dissidents in Russia have learnt. At the same time the organization which cannot contrive to accommodate the questioning mind in its midst will either ossify or stumble into the most unnecessary blunders – probably both.

The elements of action-oriented thinking

I wish I knew a less clumsy adjective than 'action-oriented' to describe the type of thinking needed to increase the effectiveness of marketing management's role in the healthy development of an organization. But clumsy or not, it does encapsulate the practical dilemma of the person in the marketing hot seat. The contribution of most of the traditional management functions is highly visible. Production has volume and cost targets to be measured by. Sales too has targets to meet, and tends to resent the Johnny-come-lately marketing function. Personnel hires people who work out or don't work out and keeps staff turnover within bounds. Finance – well, money is at the centre of everything, the ultimate measure if not the root cause. But what does marketing do, except spend a lot of money on research (whose results everybody knows already if they confirm their own prejudices or disbelieves if they conflict with them) and on advertising (which everybody could do better if it was left to them)? To justify his existence the marketing protagonist must be seen to make things happen; but unless he thinks very hard and persuades others to think as well, they will probably be the wrong things. Hence 'action-oriented' thinking.

The elements of this thinking all trace back to the phrase 'a questioning mind'. In every area where marketing is involved it is essential to ask questions, think of alternative answers, explore the additional questions that these answers provoke, and so on. The process starts with one of marketing's primary responsibilities – gathering and analysing market information. In itself information is innocuous and can be ignored by those who prefer a comfortable life while it lasts. ('There's a landmine five miles down the road.' 'So what? I don't believe it.') It is only when people start asking questions about the information and thinking about consequences that it becomes significant and worth the cost of its acquisition. How will it affect us? What problems is it likely to create? How can we convert the problems into opportunities? How much will it cost and will it be worth it? How will our customers react? And our competitors? If one way, what do we do about that? If another way, what about that? And so on.

This line of argument can sound like an invitation to do more and more research without ever reaching a decision to do anything. It very often happens in conditions of short-termitis. Governments with only a couple of years to run have been known to set up commissions of inquiry as a device for dumping a knotty problem in the laps of their successors. Chief executives in the last years of a glorious reign, studded with honours and profit-sharing bonuses, have been known to bequeath to their successors expensive long-term decisions about overdue adjustment to change. It is not easy to overcome the self-preserving motivation from which such procrastination arises. But a final question that the marketing protagonist should always ask is 'When?' In a changing competitive environment, a 'window of opportunity' is usually open for only a limited period. If you're too late (or for that matter too early) you might as well not bother. This should put a term to endless research and underline the fact that at some point thinking analytically and creatively about the information you already have will be more useful (as well as less time consuming) than acquiring more and yet more information.

Inventing marketable concepts

The qualifying adverbs 'analytically' and 'creatively' are used very deliberately about the thinking that should follow the collection of information, because a judicious mix of the two rather different types of thinking is essential if more than partial success is to be achieved.

The analytical approach is necessary in order to ensure that all the factors relevant to the organization's decision-making and forward planning have been synthesized and the key factors identified. Too often catastrophic decisions are made because too much emphasis has been put on certain factors – a technological breakthrough, an unexpected acquisition opportunity, a fall in raw material prices, a change in government fiscal policy, an identified gap in the market – without balanced analysis of the whole picture, both short term and long term. The history of business and social development initiatives is studded with foreseeable failures because the facts were not fully investigated and their implications not fully thought through. Heavy chemical factories are built at great expense to meet an immediate market shortage, which has disappeared by the time they have come on stream – either because the components of demand and impending technological change at user level had not been sufficiently investigated, or because several competitors identified and rushed to fill a market gap in which there was room for only one or two. Fortunes and the lives of individuals have been invested in backing technological developments without sufficient thought about the resources needed to market them, or whether – given the present speed of technology transfer – more powerful competitors would have acquired the technology before customer demand had risen to economic levels (the story of hovercraft and many other British inventions). Social initiatives, like the regeneration of inner cities, are embarked on and abandoned because the resources and the time required to produce results – and most particularly the difficulty of changing people's attitudes – have not been analysed and accepted.

But in a competitive world – and ultimately no organization, whether governmental, multinational or monopolistic, is free from some form of competition – the most comprehensive and far-sighted of analytical thinking is insufficient by itself. One reason for this has already been hinted at. Six different people in competitive organizations thinking analytically about the same problem are likely to reach much the same conclusion – particularly if, as so often in the States, they have all come out of Harvard Business School – and there is probably not room for six angels to dance on that particular pin. The second reason is that the obvious solution arrived at by analytical reasoning tends to be pretty boring. To catch people's imagination and secure the vital support of colleagues and customers requires a spark of imagination, an element of creative originality that is more than simply cosmetic. The analytical and the creative cast of mind seldom cohabit in the same skull. But it should be possible to bring them together in the same organization.

Foreseeing consequences

Foreseeing consequences is another aspect of organizational think-ing that tends to be neglected because of the glamour and the rewards attending the man of action, the curse of short-termitis and the widespread belief that the future is unpredictable. So it is, up to a point. But the degree of unpredictability is greatly exaggerated; and difficult though it may be, prediction obviously has to be attempted in any situation where today's decision pays off (or fails to do so) at some point in the future. My farming neighbour is relieved by the kindly bureaucrats in Brussels, with their intervention prices, from deciding when and where to ship his grain; but deciding whether to take his piglets to market today or feed them for another couple of weeks is an inescapable exercise in predicting market conditions. So is the village shopkeeper's decision on how much to buy of the wholesaler's special offer. And so at another level of time and money (and political pressures) is the Central Electricity Generating Board's decision whether to build another nuclear energy plant to come on stream in ten years' time. How far prediction can be left to the mathematician and the computer and how far it demands a thinking input will be discussed in the next chapter.

Contingency planning

The dilemma that consistently accurate prediction is impossible, but the attempt to predict inescapable, is partly resolved by contingency planning. This too demands its tribute of analytical and creative thinking. 'What happens if . . .' is the key question here, with the choice of the ifs depending as much on experience as on the extremes of optimistic or pessimistic imagination. In competitive marketing, experience will usually give you a shrewd idea of how rival concerns will react to your initiatives (though occasionally they may surprise you). In the financial services industry, competitors will probably imitate your new product or service as fast as they can get round to it. In fast moving consumer goods, depending on their corporate personalities, they may try to strangle your new product at birth by undercutting its price; or they may watch what you do and, if you are successful, follow you into the marketplace with something bigger and better. Such contingencies can be foreseen and thought through. The economic and political environment is probably less predictable, but it is not too hard to think about the best and the worst that can happen, and plan accordingly. The most important factor of all, the reaction of the consuming public, can be predicted – given intelligent analysis of research findings – with considerable accuracy; and once again variations in either direction from the expected can be planned for.

Monitoring, adjusting, improving

This is a fourth area of action-oriented thinking that is often neglected by the men and women of action. In all organizations – whether they be governments grappling with the intricacies of economic management, or toiletry manufacturers spawning new devices to make ladies and gents feel more attractive than nature intended – there is an almost irresistible temptation to stop thinking and grasshopper off to other activities when what looks like the right formula has been found. 'Monetarism, that's the answer, let's stick to it.' 'Brylcreem, that's the answer (and a sticky one too); lets stick to it.' It may be the right answer for a short time; but the lifetime of the product or the policy in a changing world will be shorter than it need have been if its protagonists, prime ministers and product managers alike, fail to keep on thinking, watching and adjusting. There will always be a better way of doing it next year or the year after.

Organizing for effective thinking

No serious organization watcher can fail to recognize the widespread disease of being too busy to have time to think. But it would be unfair to deny that many organizations are beginning to think hard about how to think better.

Organizational devices to create a more congenial environment for action-oriented thinking, like government think-tanks and corporate project task forces, can be effective in the right circumstances. In the wrong circumstances (distressingly frequent) they can deteriorate into obedient search parties, dedicated to the pursuit of arguments to justify the preconceptions of their masters; or into ornamental status symbols, designed to demonstrate that we too can intellectualize, but divorced from the mainstream of organizational life. It is more likely to produce effective action if, instead of or as well as the think-tanks and task forces, there are virulent centres of thinking infection in all the major limbs and organs of the corporate body; and these centres are linked, both formally and informally, by the kind of intelligent liaison that recognizes the interdependence of the total organism.

Other organizational devices like brainstorming sessions and creative circles can also play a constructive part in making the thinking power of an organization far greater than that of any individual, however brilliant. But two provisos have to be made if organized thinking is to be more than an empty pantomime. The first is that the organization must be prepared to season the pot of organization men, whom all personnel departments and functional managers prefer, by recruiting and retaining a sprinkling of those awkward characters who are constantly out of step and given to emulating Hans Andersen's small boy by saying out loud that the Emperor has no clothes. The second proviso is that there is positive encouragement, from the top down, of original thinking and innovative ideas, however crazy they may seem (or actually turn out to be).

How far does marketing's responsibility extend in enhancing the organization's thinking power and performance? It would be ludicrous for any marketing manager or marketing department to aspire to the title of organizational brain. From the very practical viewpoint of survival in organizations where visible results count, it would be singularly imprudent to neglect entirely the pursuit of short-term successes in favour of long-range thinking; from the more objective viewpoint of balanced, comprehensive thinking that leads to action, it is clearly important that all sectors of the organization should contribute to the thinking as well as the doing. But there is a strong argument for holding that marketing, if not in the lead, should play a major part in all development thinking. Marketing, the argument runs, is the function most closely in touch with the customers, and if the customer says it's a rotten idea then for all practical purposes that's it.

Part Two

Managing Change

'Any change, even for the better, is to be deprecated' is a sentiment that has been attributed, no doubt falsely, to the American military establishment. It is certainly rife among well-organized commercial and governmental establishments in this country – the better organized, the rifer – for very obvious reasons. It is difficult enough to cope with today's crises, let alone those which may never happen in an uncertain tomorrow; in the happy moments when everything seems at last to be under control, the forward thinker who suggests that the new plant or the new organization structure that is only just run in needs to be changed will not be popular.

Yet constant – and constantly accelerating – change is an inescapable feature of developed and developing countries; and any organization that fails to recognize this and change as fast as its environment will suffer, if not complete collapse, the humiliation of takeover or subservience to more progressive societies. One of the less popular responsibilities of the marketing function, in closer touch by definition with external events and the pressures of competition, is to keep pointing this out and pressing for action. In seeking to keep the corporate craft from running on to the reef ahead, marketers lay themselves open to accusations of rocking the boat.

The devices open to the bureaucracy for frustrating efforts to bring about change – for the better – tend to revolve around a few dismissive and not always ill-founded objections. 'You keep talking about the major problems and opportunities that you foresee; I haven't noticed that dramatic business and economic forecasts like yours are all that reliable. Why should we disturb a smoothly running business to satisfy your idiosyncratic vision of the future?' 'That's a very plausible plan that you've put up. But those of us with more practical experience than you know only too well that things very rarely go according to plan.' 'We don't seem to have the knack of dreaming up bright new ideas that actually work.' 'Look at all the new projects we got into that flopped.'

Attitudes like these, reinforced by the dead weight of natural inertia, are not easy to deal with – except when the situation is so desperate that people will try anything (usually too late). This part of the book looks at ways in which the marketing-oriented chief executive or the marketing manager who accepts his responsibility for managing change – or with any luck the two in partnership – can make it less difficult to overcome the resistances; it will never be easy.

8 The clouded crystal ball

'Every decision in life rests upon a forecast.' So says one well-known forecaster, correctly enough. The decision to take or not to take an umbrella to work today is based on a forecast about the weather, qualified by the risk of leaving said brolly on the train. So is the decision of the tour operator on whether or not to charter the marginal plane for a flight to Majorca or to reserve the marginal hotel room; the level of profit or loss for the operator is directly related to the number of seats and beds, filled on the day or night of truth – which in its turn will be affected by such factors as exchange rates, fuel costs, the weather, competitive pricing, changes in disposable income, the incidence of terrorism, and whether or not the hotel gets built in time.

Not all of these factors – or the factors affecting other decisions – can be predicted with any certainty. Competitors may unexpectedly start a price war; politicians, sadly oblivious of the interests of the tourist industry, may take decisions that upset all predictions about exchange rates; bombs may go off at the most inconvenient time and place. The temptation is to say that all forecasts are wrong (which up to a point they mostly are), so we will concentrate on today's problems and rely on the notorious British talent for improvisation to look after tomorrow.

Clearly the refusal to forecast and plan ahead is as unsatisfactory as an uncritical acceptance of the forecasters' reliability. Those who refuse to plan ahead are, in fact, making the implicit forecast that next year will be much the same as this year; and that's a forecast which in an epoch of accelerating change is bound to be wrong. The only sensible policy is to make the best fist of forecasting you can, hedge your bets with a strong infusion of contingency planning and risk evaluation, work towards a progressive improvement in forecasting accuracy – as long as the cost of increased accuracy does not outweigh the benefit – and avoid the most obvious mistakes. I would be embarrassed to propound so simplistic a formula, if I hadn't seen so many organizations, large and small, suffer from disregarding it.

The wishful thinking forecast

One of the most obvious (and frequent) mistakes is to make a wholly unrealistic forecast, even to believe it, just because it would be highly convenient if it should actually come true. This happens when a growth company, which has been able to boast for years to shareholders and investment analysts that each year's sales and profits were ahead of last year's, hits a bad patch or begins to run out of steam. The pressure builds up down the line – with the marketing department always a primary target – to add just a few percentage points to the sales forecasts (well within the margin of error, of course), to raise prices a little more than is prudent (the customers won't notice a few pennies more with everything going up), or to launch a new product before it has been properly tested. It would be unrealistic to deny that more can be squeezed out of the marketing orange in an emergency, but to do it habitually or in a hurry invites catastrophe.

A sales forecast designed to keep a plant or a major piece of equipment running at optimum efficiency can also be born of wishful thinking if it is well adrift of any reasonable forecast of what can actually be sold. But here there is room for considerable give and take. If the break-even point for a given plant really is 90 per cent of capacity, it is as unhelpful for the marketing manager to say 'Sorry, there's no hope of selling that amount next year' and let it go at that, as it is to make over-optimistic promises that he cannot honour. He is entitled as a member of management to demand economies in the factory that will reduce break-even point and give the company more room for manoeuvre; but he is bound also to seek new outlets in home or export markets, and to devise price or promotional stratagems that will help to close the gap from his end.

A sales and profit forecast designed primarily to justify a new investment or an acquisition (or to fight off a predator) can also arise from wishful thinking – if not worse. This has happened too often in the past in development areas, where government agencies dedicated to the cause of increased employment have handed over large sums of taxpayers' money to entrepreneurs promising to create jobs. The promises as a rule checked out at least in the short run. Yes, it would take so many men to build the green field factory, so many men and women to run the plant and the office; and of course spin-off jobs would be created in the local service industries. What would seldom be worked out in enough detail to satisfy the most mildly critical eye was just how the product – electronic gadgets, sports cars or whatever it might be – would be brought to market and sold at a profit. After an embarrassing number of short-lived episodes, development agencies began to accept that the crucial question in any investment proposal is not whether Britain can make it, but whether Britain can sell it; and to insist on realistic marketing plans as well as production plans.

One-dimensional forecasting

As misleading as wishful thinking is the forecast based primarily on a single factor with which the forecaster is preoccupied. This seems so obvious that it is scarcely worth stating – except that it keeps happening. Not long ago one of the leading international manufacturers of metal containers, the happy possessor of a particularly strong R & D department, developed a new type of container which combined lower manufacturing costs with greater suitability for storing chemicals and other user products. Factories were geared up to make the new containers, whose sales potential could readily be forecast by totting up the output of customers whose products (and costs) would benefit from the development; before very long the new plants had to be ungeared to the accompaniment of painful redundancies. The trouble was that the company's marketing department was much less strong and much less influential in the company's corridors of power than the R & D department. The fact had been overlooked that customers need to be persuaded to change their packing methods, taking time to adjust to the idea and more time to carry out their own tests; as had the fact that the user industries, for which the new container was most suitable, were entering a downturn in their economic cycle, with reduced turnover and diminished inclination to try anything new.

So is marketing always the victim, never the villain of uni-dimensional forecasting failures? By no means. Every experienced marketing man's conscience is burdened with occasions when he forgot some relevant factor that made nonsense of his predictions. There was the head of an advertising agency's media department who was carried away, in the early days of colour TV, by the results of consumer research, reporting the enthusiasm of the new owners of colour sets and the envy of the majority who still had black and white sets. He visited all the agency's major clients advising them that within a year 50 per cent of homes would have colour sets, so they should make all their commercials in colour. A year later he made the rounds of the same clients, now somewhat disgruntled by the poor return on their TV advertising investment, to make a clean breast of it. 'A year ago I forecast that by now 50 per cent of homes would have colour TV. The actual figure turns out to be less than a third of this, because I failed to realize that set manufacturers would have teething troubles, making it impossible for them to satisfy demand. Now I would like to say goodbye to all my ex-friends, my boss having failed to disagree with my decision to seek fresh employment.'

And there was the marketing planner for a firm of canned baby food manufacturers who drew the logical conclusion from a declining birthrate that next year's sales would be down on this year's; fewer infant mouths for parents to aim at, *ergo* lower sales. But sales did not decline because the falling trend of births was offset by a rising tide of medical opinion in favour of switching sooner from milk to solid foods.

Forecasting has been a problem throughout recorded history, starting with the semi-religious practice of consulting the oracle or the auspices. The Delphi oracle set the precedent, followed by many modern economists, of avoiding error by combining an excellent intelligence service, a handsome system of payment by anxious enquirers, and a studied ambiguity of response. It was the priestess at Delphi, seated on her tripod and wreathed in intoxicating fumes, who told the unfortunate Croesus, king of Lydia, that if he went to war with Persia he would destroy a great kingdom; when he found, defeated and captured, that it was his own kingdom that was destroyed it was too late to get his money back.

Marketing men who yearn to build a reputation for infallible forecasting would be best advised to go into the futurology business. Forecasting the shape of things twenty-odd years ahead (the year 2000, that hardy date, is getting a bit close, so it may soon have to be 2020, tying up with 20/20 vision) allows scope for imaginative flights of fancy to enliven the pedestrian projection of trends; and it has the added advantage that when the day of reckoning arrives, nobody will bother to check how wrong you were.

The pragmatic approach

For practising managers and marketers, who have to forecast the actual sales of actual products and the net sales revenue that will be generated – and have to stand by their predictions – a systematic approach to the reduction of uncertainty is likely to be the best course. If the factors affecting a future situation are analysed, it will become evident that some are more significant than others, some more predictable than others and some more controllable than others. Aggregate customer demand – itself a function of customer numbers, purchasing power and propensity to purchase – is highly significant in most cases. Customer numbers should be very predictable, once the target customer segment has been defined; year-on-year changes are unlikely to be great. Purchasing power can be slightly harder to predict but, unless the customer base is uncomfortably small, averages will help; one customer may unexpectedly go bust, but it is unlikely that many will simultaneously get into difficulties without some early warning signs.

The greatest uncertainty lies in the factor of propensity to purchase, particularly propensity to purchase from you rather than your competitors. Here the marketer's research tools can help to reduce uncertainty. These include (as any marketing textbook will confirm) surveys of buyer intentions, surveys of sales force opinion, surveys of expert opinion and test markets. Each has its pros and cons and none is infallible; but when two or more are used in conjunction – and taken with a pinch of experienced salt – they will make the marketing oracle's forecast a good deal more informed. *Surveys of buyer intentions* have proved, unsurprisingly, most reliable for serious purchases that tend to be planned, like industrial equipment and consumer durables; and highly unreliable for products and services in the impulse purchase category. For the latter, deduction from previous behaviour is likely to give better results. *Sales force opinion* is useful because salesmen who are good at their job will have a feel for customer attitudes and intentions; but experienced marketing managers will learn to adjust their figures in the light of individual characteristics – the optimists whose eyes are always bigger than their order forms, and the canny ones who calculate that the secret of a happy life is always to beat your targets and who forecast accordingly. *Expert opinion* is most helpful when the experts, like motorcar and equipment distributors or investment fund managers, are themselves actively involved in the market and by their own behaviour make it more likely that their prophecies will come true. *Test markets* are in many ways the most reliable aid to more accurate forecasts, conforming as they do to that refined scientific principle 'Suck it and see.' But they have certain disadvantages. They take time, which may result, when the situation is rapidly changing, in missing the most favourable tide. They alert competitors to your intentions, allowing them to learn almost as much from your experiment as you do yourself. And while in theory the test is an exact microcosm of the eventual broad-scale project, the change in time, place and scale mean that the latter in practice can never exactly reproduce the former.

Projecting the past into the future

Field research, designed to reduce uncertainty, costs money; and the degree to which it is reduced, as well as the degree of risk involved in being badly wrong, need to be large enough to justify the cost. When there are significant factors involved, with reliable records from the past that can be charted and show significant trend patterns, it is wise to supplement field research with projected trends from the past; and it is tempting to rely on them exclusively. Given enough data from the past, it is possible to develop mathematical formulae that will predict sales of a given product or commodity with some reliability, other things being equal – like the formula published in 1964 by an industrious academic, which would have enabled anyone sufficiently interested and far-sighted to predict sales of Lydia Pinkham's Vegetable Compound between 1908 and 1960 rather accurately.

The catch lies in the saving phrase 'other things being equal' – which being interpreted usually means 'provided that history repeats itself', a proviso that it would be imprudent to count on. Too many trend lines, even those sophisticated versions that allow for seasonal variations, trade cycles, price inflation and the like, have been shattered by some unforeseen event that played no part in the normal pattern of the past – an event on a macro-scale like the formation of OPEC and the consequent revolution in energy prices, or on a micro-scale like a competitor catching you on the hop with an unforeseen new product launch or promotional ploy.

Unforeseen, yes. Unforeseeable, no. In both cases it would have been possible to predict, through a probing survey of informed opinion or even by sitting and thinking, that the owners of a valuable commodity would eventually stop selling it below its market value; or to hear the faint rumble of coming events. Even in markets that have been apparently stable and pedictable in the past the pragmatic forecaster will not rely wholly on his computer model or his chartists, but encourage his colleagues to devote some time to the leading edge of dreams or nightmares. What could happen to make things turn out far better or far worse than might reasonably be expected? The forecaster, after all the niggling adjustments that realistic multidimensional forecasting demands, must stick his neck out and settle on statements and figures that reflect the most probable outcome of future events; but this idea does not debar him from adding 'best case' and 'worst case' forecasts that his colleagues, the corporate and marketing planners, can use as the basis of contingency plans. In this case (or indeed if only one forecast is proffered) the assumptions on which the forecast is based need to be stated, so that contingency plans can be activated rapidly, if the unlikely assumptions come to pass or the likely ones turn out to be wrong.

Controllability

An aspect of forecasting that is sometimes overlooked is the self-fulfilling prophecy, or more precisely the extent to which the view of the future taken by a powerful player affects that future. The nearer a market comes to monopoly or oligopoly, the greater the effect will be. It can be seen among the clearing banks, where competition among the big four who dominate the market tends to take the form of rapidly following each other's initiatives. (This is not, incidentally, a question of a surreptitious cartel, but simply acknowledges the fact that failure to follow suit leads as a rule to loss of business.) The sequence of events can be imagined. The forward planners in one of the banks foresee that say within a year they will all be offering private customers who stay in credit a free banking service. So the decision is made to gain the advantage of being first to make the offer. So the other three follow suit. So the original forecaster got it right. Congratulations.

In practice the controllability factor operates to some extent in almost every forecasting situation, starting with the individual who may not be master of his fate from the time he closes his front gate to go to work, but can control to a great extent the degree to which his garden next year produces flowers, vegetables or simply weeds. For an organization there are usually circles of controllability, from an inner circle where control of the future is almost absolute to outer circles (product categories in which the organization has only a minor share, export markets it has barely entered) where control is minimal. The marketing planner seeking to reduce uncertainty will be well advised to include in his composite forecast sufficient high-control components to provide a stable base.

Forecasters at work

The ideal marketing forecaster – if the ideal anyone were any more of a reality than the average anyone – would be found somewhere on the continuum between the purely objective observer, armed with his computer and his forecasting model, and the sensitive adjudicator, involved in the practical world where logic and reason are not the only factors that shape events, who is capable of assembling evidence from a variety of sources and reaching a balanced judgement; even the hunch merchants who feel it in their bones may in fact be going unconsciously through the latter process.

If the last paragraph betrays some personal prejudice against the 'scientific' and mathematical end of the forecasting continuum, it is a consequence of observing and participating in the forecasting activities of many different organizations. Few pay as much attention to this activity as is demanded by the fact that the outcome of this year's management decisions is very largely determined by next month's or next year's or the next five years' market climate. But this apart it is notable that results come closer to forecasts when those responsible for the forecasts, whether as product managers or as divisional managers, are accountable for making them come true than when they are produced in an ivory tower planning department. This is not to deny that the chief executive of a far-flung organization will be well advised to have his own forecasting capability to provide some insurance against his proconsuls' forecasts becoming either too ambitious or too cosily conservative.

Wherever the forecasting responsibility is located, the ideal forecaster of my dreams – alas, I have yet to meet him or her – will, if not a marketer by calling, have some of the marketer's feeling for customers, voters or whoever in the final analysis calls the tune; and will be in a position to use some of the market research tools for reducing uncertainty. The forecasting team (it may be a group with diverse skills and backgrounds or a single individual calling on part-time contributions from others) will develop a sceptical balance between projections from past experience into the future and the kind of imaginative hunch that is more than just day-dreaming. It will have analysed and taken into account all the diverse factors that can be expected to affect the pattern of the future, and will also allow room in its forecasts for the unexpected. For the latter purpose it may well accept – with reservations – the advice of outside advisers, including the futurologists. They may lack the disciplines of the organizational forecaster, who is only too well aware of the constraints of the status quo and the practical obstacles to dramatic change; but for the same reason they can be less inhibited in their thinking.

The team will be very conscious of the degree of controllability in certain areas of their forecasts and the degree to which conviction on the part of those accountable for performance can affect the outcome. So those team members who are not anchored to their computer terminals will be at pains to discuss the development of their forecasts with the implementers.

Having done all the right things, the team will still get it more or less wrong. So it has learned to be humble without being mealy-mouthed. While it makes firm forecasts of the most likely outcome, it also provides the planners with forecasts of what might happen in the best and worst case as a basis for contingency plans. It also recognizes the increasing unreliability of forecasts as they move further into the future (apart from Keynes's irrefutable statement that in the long run we are all dead) and seeks to forecast no further ahead than is necessary for managerial decision-making; when long-term forecasts are needed, as in the case of major capital investments designed to pay off in the distant future, it attempts to estimate the margin of error.

The team also regularly revises its forecasts in the light of actual events. This gives the curious illusion that forecasts are never wrong, since the correct figures are substituted for the incorrect as soon as the facts are out. In practice changes are not made lightheartedly, but are accompanied by an explanation of the cause. When the cause is a controllable variable, appropriate action is taken by management; when it is uncontrollable the forecasters learn something from their mistake and seek to do better next time. Or the time after that. Perfection is never attainable, but its pursuit is a very rewarding exercise.

9 Planning into action

If this were a well-ordered world – ideally ordered by a marketing man – marketing's contribution to planning and its conversion into action would have been one of the main battle honours won by the profession over the last thirty years. The logic, derived from such adages as 'Look before you leap', appears irrefutable. Collecting relevant facts about the present and forecasting the future environment (an area in which marketing can claim some expertise) is an essential preliminary to planning. The plan, which needs to take full account of marketing's special interest, the customer, is a sensible preliminary to action. Action, preferably the right action – or sometimes deliberate inaction – is the ultimate justification for the whole process; and the technique, claimed by marketing, of product management can help to ensure that the action actually takes place, more or less on time.

Yet for the most part the apparently predictable planning triumphs of marketing have not gone according to plan. There are certainly some companies, mostly in fast moving consumer goods, where the annual marketing plan, with its regular revisions, is the blueprint for the organization's future, with production and even financial plans following respectfully in its wake. Tiny Tots' Toys Ltd, for example, a small family business struggling to survive in a harsh world where large suppliers are congenitally reluctant to extend credit and large customers equally reluctant to pay their bills on time, were in no doubt that life began (and could end) with their marketing plan for the Christmas season. Prediction is never easy in the toy industry, because of its traditional seasonality, cramming half the year's retail sales into the last couple of months, and increasingly because of the fashion element whereby this year's best seller may be dead by next year. But the trade fairs at the beginning of the year, at which few firm orders are placed, give some indication of distributors' reactions to a company's offerings; and the economic forecasters give some indication of whether it will be a free-spending or an impoverished Christmas.

So Tiny Tots' Toys make their sales forecasts at the beginning of the year, doing what they can to ensure that they will come true by interspersing the fashion items in their product range with some reliable old favourites like teddy bears, by carefully scheduling delivery dates along critical path lines, and by planning what they hope will be an effective promotional campaign within the limits of affordability. At the same time they watch such indicators as early orders, prepared to adjust their forecasts upwards or downwards if (as they inevitably will) sales of individual lines exceed or fall short of expectations.

Production plans follow from the marketing plan, or in real time precede it, since skilled labour and expensive plant are both more cost-effective if worked evenly round the year than if oscillating between idleness and overtime. Financial planning also has to follow the marketing flag, since building up stocks in the early part of the year requires finance; and bank managers are cautious about accepting stocks that may or may not be saleable as security for loans.

It cannot be said that Tiny Tots' marketing plan is a model for the textbooks; with a slim management team, it is more of a back-of-an-envelope job than a fat and formal document. Things do not always work out as planned. In good years there are holidays in the sun and bonuses all round; in bad years it can be a lean Christmas. But there can be no doubt that lacking any plan the company would collapse.

The National Bank of Mudshire is a quite different case. Like all large banks it is rich in market information – not always as easily retrievable or widely disseminated as it might be. Practical experience of investing in new computer systems, overseas branch openings, acquisitions and other costly long-term projects has convinced its senior managers – if they needed convincing, being very practical men – that planning ahead is important. Because the bank can afford to buy the best advisers its planning procedures, worked out in consultation with a bevy of business school professors, follow the most up-to-date scientific principles.

The bank operates a planning cycle – aptly named because it rolls on and on without intermission, like a fairground big wheel. The annual cycle begins in January of each year when the central planning group takes counsel with itself about the likely economic climate in the year starting twelve months later and about the stage which the bank's long-term development projects should have reached by then. Based on this review the unit drafts around Easter a chief executive's letter of guidance to the heads of the operating divisions, setting out in general terms the bank's objectives for the following year and the part which each division is expected to play in it. There follows a period of toing and froing between the central planners and the divisional planners, during which efforts are made to reconcile the theoretical with the practical. When there are arguments they are usually won by the spokesmen for the operating divisions, who are seldom slow to point out that they represent profit centres which actually earn the cash that the central planners use to fuel their paper factory.

From then on there is little the central planning unit can do except wait for the divisions' operational plans to be completed and then cobble them together into a corporate plan (now accompanied by a budget) which with luck will bear some resemblance in its detailed exposition of the first year to the main burden of the chief executive's original letter of guidance. Outline plans for the three subsequent years, which are included, are much less of a problem; nobody is committed yet to carrying them out, so compromise with the ideal is unnecessary.

By the beginning of December everything is ready for a celebratory management meeting to promulgate the charted high-lights of the plan (whose written version by now is so bulky a document that nobody of any importance has time to read it in full) and its authors are liberated for their round of Christmas parties before re-embarking in January on the next revolution of the big wheel.

The finer points of Mudshire's planning procedures, which really are a model of their kind, have probably been missed in this cursory account. What is disturbing about the process – and the similar processes followed by other large organizations – is that the many man-hours of honest toil involved do not appear to have any significant effect on the course of events. Decisions are made at all levels, often rather late in the day, not because they were planned in advance, but because some emergency occurred – some initiative by a competitor, a customer in trouble, an economic crisis abroad, an internal operating bottleneck – which demanded an appropriate reaction. 'Why are we always the reactive bridesmaid, never the proactive bride?' is the constant complaint of worried managers, as the planning cycle rolls ponderously on.

What worries the critics most is the fragility of the connection between plan and subsequent action in the case of the Mudshire corporate plan and others like it. The marketing propagandist would say that this is because the planning system is too intro-verted, paying more attention in its conception to the needs of the organization, expressed in terms of manpower, premises, tech-nology and investment, than to the predicted needs of the customer and predictable changes in the market. There is some truth in this. Because it is only beginning to be recognized that marketing has an important role to play in banking (as in government and other organizational activities which need to pay more attention to people and their idiosyncrasies) the marketing input arrives rather late in the proceedings – at the stage of tactical implementation rather than strategic concepts.

Just as important as the gap between plan and action is the cultural gap between the congenital planners, who have their holidays and their careers mapped out months or years in advance, and the congenital improvisers, who believe that each day's events are unpredictable and pride themselves on their ability to cope with whatever turns up when it happens. Perhaps regrettably it is the latter who usually win out; it was Harold Wilson with his 'One week in politics is a long time' who became Prime Minister, and George Brown, his erstwhile rival, whose national plan was laughed out of court. Our national distaste for planning – almost a point of false pride when we boast of losing every battle but the last and of inventing things for others to exploit – is ceasing to be affordable as we sink lower in the international pecking order.

But there's more to it than that. The planners invite the disregard of the doers when they adopt an excessively elaborate and inflexible approach to their craft. Given the one certainty about forecasts of the future – that they will be wrong in some respects, and the further away in time or space the greater the error – it is futile to plan in great detail for a scenario that will have changed, perhaps out of all recognition, by the time it arrives. The right compromise between a modest degree of flexibility that leaves room for manoeuvre and an excessive degree that makes nonsense of the discipline that planning should impose has to be a matter of individual judgement. Certainly the company whose annual sales forecasts, as I recall, were revised monthly with the actual figure substituted for the forecast without comment or demur had carried flexibility to the point of absurdity. Its forecasts by December were remarkably accurate but further adrift from the targets set at the beginning of the year than they would have been if discrepancies between plan and performance had been taken more seriously.

For determining degrees of flexibility the distinction between strategic and tactical planning, made by Mudshire among others, is important in principle. Strategy must be flexible, dealing with such fundamental questions as 'What business are we in?' – better put perhaps as 'What business do we intend to be in?' Strategic planning can set directions, calculate the build-up of resources that will be needed, forecast relevant developments in the social, economic and commercial environment and estimate time scales. But it can never be forgotten that many of the factors involved, particularly environmental and competitive developments, are partly un-predictable and wholly uncontrollable.

Tactical projects are much more controllable; indeed the probability of plan and performance more or less coinciding is greatly increased by tight control and co-ordination following a formal plan buttressed by contingency planning. So, in principle again you arrive at a happy combination of an indicative strategic plan setting general directions and a number of more precise tactical plans for advances in the general direction laid down. In *principle*; in practice there is endless scope for argument about whether a tactical plan espoused by some robber baron in an independently minded division does or does not conform with central strategy.

This, with similar discontinuities between plan and action, makes it important for those planners who find ivory tower confinement essentially futile, to spend much of their time during the preparation of their plans on securing widespread involvement among the power brokers of the organization; a plan that falls short of perfection but is generally accepted and understood is more useful than a creative masterpiece buried in the files. It is equally important to spend time on securing commitment to the completed plan on the part of all those contributing to its implementation.

Finally, if plan and action are to connect effectively individuals need to be given specific tasks and targets within the framework of the plan and to be held accountable for their achievement – which in turn requires a system of monitoring performance against target. The mechanics of this need not be a problem, if the organization's management information system is sufficiently flexible to accommodate it (sometimes a big if); but the realities of the corporate power structure make it difficult for the planners – usually lacking a power base – to take corrective action when targets are not met. Which brings the argument full circle to the chicken-and-egg proposition that unless the people at the top believe planning to be effective, it will not be effective; and unless there is an effective planning system they will not as pragmatists believe that it can be effective.

Charlie Chown, hired by Platters Ltd to add the polish of his reputed marketing expertise to their already quite profitable business, ran head-on into the problem of senior management's scepticism about the value of marketing plans. Perhaps too soon after his arrival he remarked, among other provocative statements that did not endear him to the incumbent management, that it was ludicrous to run a business without a marketing plan. His managing director, already disturbed by the requests for larger research and advertising budgets that marketing appeared to bring in its wake, asked why. 'We already have an action programme, a budget and a cash flow forecast for next year. I've told the sales force what they've got to sell. What is your fine marketing plan going to add – apart from demands for a planning assistant and a still larger budget? Write me a paper to say what you propose and justify it on cost–benefit grounds.'

This, thought Charlie, should be a doddle. Consult any good marketing textbook for a standard marketing plan format and rationale, change the names to fit the world of Platters, and there you are. Take the excellent Kotler in *Marketing Management: Analysis, Planning and Control* (Prentice Hall): 'a logical way to proceed – diagnosis, prognosis, objectives, strategy, tactics, control', that's straightforward enough. But what is this? 'At least five different types of company planning activity can be distinguished – long-range planning, annual planning, product planning, venture planning, activity planning'; each, it seems with its own complications of model-building, charting, decision trees and algebraic equations. That is not likely to satisfy the men of action at the head of Platters, who consider one half-sheet of paper excessively verbose.

Better start again with examples of the disasters awaiting organizations that fail to pay proper attention to the planning process and the triumphs in store for those that do:

Although all firms plan, they vary considerably in how extensively, thoroughly and formally they do it. Some managements are so embroiled in daily operations that they give little time to long-range thinking, let alone planning. [That's Platters, all right.] ... Other managements go through the motions of some formal planning; written plans are prepared by individual departments, bound together, and filed away. Finally, some managements go through a full-fledged formal planning procedure, utilizing planning staff, planning committees, and written documents. These firms are convinced that formal planning is the key to corporate survival in a world of rapid social change and intense competition.

Hear, hear! But what is this? 'Conclusive evidence is lacking that firms that do the most planning fare substantially better than the rest because of their planning.' Dear Professor, that's a big help – like telling me that if I study the scriptures, do good deeds and give all that I have to the poor, I'll probably burn in hell just the same.

So Charlie, out on his own again, considers the art of the possible in Platters. Should he retreat gracefully, saying that on reflection, when things are going so well and such crises as do arise are being dealt with so expeditiously, he would be reluctant to rock the boat? Or should he confine his planning proposals to the more manageable field of product management, seeking to demonstrate on a smaller scale that a meticulously planned operation is more likely to succeed than a sudden brainwave followed by a series of energetic improvisations?

Charlie was one of those people – certainly a majority of articulate human beings – who find it difficult to develop their thoughts within the privacy of their own skulls. His most imaginative, cogently argued plans and proposals were the outcome of discussions with colleagues, both supporters and opponents, committed to paper and rigorously revised. There was nobody he could talk freely to at Platters. But at least there was paper to spare. So, to sort out his thoughts, he put on paper – or rather on the screen of his word processor, a memento of his brief spell as blue-eyed boy of the organization – what he described as:

A dialogue between myself as devil's advocate (DA) and myself as starry-eyed idealist (SEI)

DA   What real good will it do to this lot, if I persuade them to take planning, specifically marketing planning, more seriously?

SEI   On the company policy level, three potential benefits, each with a big if against it. The company, it seems to me, has reached a stage of somewhat complacent middle age. The first impulse that got it started, the excitement of youth, has faded. It will sink into arthritic old age, if the people at the top don't periodically take time out to look at the changing world around them and see what new products or services they should be developing to replace the ones that are doomed to die. The itch to innovate can be the first benefit.

A second benefit is that icebergs ahead can be avoided more easily if the evasive action is taken early on and if your radar system is in good working order. The third is that any action is more likely to succeed if all the ingredients of success are clearly defined and specified individuals made accountable for each of them.

DA   Fine soapbox stuff. And how do you expect to persuade the chief executive, who is already rehearsing his excuses for the next AGM (another difficult year, despite which we succeeded in improving our net profits by almost 2 per cent), to transfer resources from ageing products that can still be milked for a profit to new products or initiatives that will be expensive to start with and may never show a profit?

SEI   If he doesn't, the business will be dead in ten years.

DA   By which time he will have been retired for seven years.

SEI   Well, then, let's put the frighteners on. If we don't anticipate our customers' changing needs and make plans to meet them, more far-sighted competitors will take business away from us.

DA When we see that happening we'll lay on a crash programme to get it back. Let them do the planning and the pioneering. We'll just copy their successes and avoid their mistakes.

SEI Crash programmes are expensive.

DA So are elaborate plans to deal with events that may never happen.

SEI But I believe that sensible planning, closely related to this company's objectives and resources, is bound both to save money and to make money.

DA Your faith will get you a long way, to martyrdom perhaps, if you are the only true believer in a bunch of infidels. How are you going to convert them? They don't seem very responsive to sermons.

SEI Perhaps I should begin again, by looking at the theoretical benefits of formal planning procedures and work out how a start might be made towards them, without getting trampled to death by the anti-planners – the first steps so to speak in a marketing plan for the infiltration of planning. At the corporate level I suppose the key benefit is the occasion formal planning provides for management to get away from their daily preoccupations and think more comprehensively about what is going on in the world around them and where the organization is heading; and to make their dispositions accordingly.

DA Do you need an elaborate planning system to make that happen? Remember you have a mandate to improve the organization's management information system. Could you not use that as an excuse to produce an annual 'State of the market' report (like the US President's state of the nation report) for the chief executive to discuss with management? If you pulled together desk research, such continuing customer research as you have, and internal statistics, and seasoned it with a respectful sprinkling of senior managers' own views, you could produce a pretty stimulating – and worrying – report. People always enjoy discussing research reports, particularly when their own hobby-horses are given an airing;

and, who knows, they might get the idea that they should do something about it.

SEI   Now you're being cynical about the colleagues I know and love. It's a poor start, but perhaps the best I can do until I've established my credibility by some demonstrable marketing successes. How about the operational benefit of a planned and co-ordinated marketing project, as against an unplanned improvisation.

DA   If nothing else you should be able to get a statement or re-statement of marketing strategy out of your state of the market meeting. Can't you use that as a jumping-off point for one or two specific new products or product improvement plans, demonstrating the advantages of a tightly co-ordinated critical path approach? Better make it a product improvement if you want a success story; new products are too accident-prone.

SEI   The difficulty about that is my lack of clout. I can plan and co-ordinate the bits I'm responsible for, like market and product acceptance research, advertising, merchandising and, up to a point, pricing and packaging. But in the end these are not as critical as product formulation, scheduling and cost plus the selling effort, and physical distribution. On these I can only persuade, entreat, watch and pray.

DA   But isn't the art of persuasion supposed to be one of the key marketing skills? Obviously it will help if you can persuade the chief executive to act as your godfather. Failing this – well, you've got to start somewhere.

Charlie was not greatly cheered by his dialogue with himself. If he followed the devil's advocate line it would be five years before a proper marketing planning system was bedded into the organiz-ation. He doubted whether he, or the company, could last that long. Nevertheless, better a slow success than a fast bloody nose. He removed his lucubrations from the word processor and embarked on the preparation of the requisite half-sheet of paper, recommend-ing a first annual state of the market meeting.

10 The art of innovation

The word 'innovation' crept, by no means unintentionally, into the last chapter as one of the end products of the marketing planning process. A serious look into the future seldom fails to identify changes in customer needs, the market environment, technology or comparative cost structures that require new products or new marketing methods if the organization concerned is to survive and prosper.

Marketing has been greatly involved in this area. A forest of literature has grown up, in particular, around the subject of new product development. Techniques have been touted like gap analysis – reviewing the range of products available to meet a particular consumer need in order to find gaps which a new product might fit into – and concept testing – investigating through discussion groups, and other forms of qualitative research, consumer reactions to new product ideas before spending serious money on the production of prototypes.

Marketing service companies have been set up, specializing either in the whole process of market development from conception to birth or in some aspect of it. Internal procedures have been established and organizational structures of varying levels of complexity and durability have been built. Yet somehow actual performance has generally been disappointing. Resounding boasts from companies priding themselves on their innovativeness that 'Products contributing nearly 50 per cent of our profits did not exist ten (or maybe twenty) years ago' are balanced by complaints from similar, sometimes the same, companies that '90 per cent of new products never earn a profit'. And the appointment of new products or product development manager, even in a successful company, has become notorious as a post of danger where it is prudent to stay close to the exit and the nearest headhunter.

Why are success rates so low in a field where marketing claims are so high and marketing techniques so highly developed? It usually comes back to one or other (or all) of the top trio that I have been hammering: failure to *think* clearly and constructively; failure to *organize*, so as to encourage creativity; and failure to control the contrariness and perversity of *people*.

Thinking

Once you start thinking seriously about the subject of innovation, it becomes obvious that it is one of those portmanteau English words into which more meanings are packed than it can comfortably accommodate. Everybody, especially marketing bodies, will readily agree that readiness to innovate is of great importance to organizations of all shapes and sizes that want to survive and prosper in a changing world. But if you push the discussion a bit further in a mixed gathering it soon becomes clear that the idea of innovation which each individual has in mind will differ widely according to their interests, experience and prejudices. Some with a background and outlook derived from large organizations will have in mind major changes in technology or markets; others from a small company perspective will think instinctively of small advances or product improvements that can give them an advantage over competitors. Some will think mainly in terms of changes, large or small, or additions to the range of products or services they offer their customers; others will instinctively put more emphasis on changes in the delivery system – the way products or services are transmitted to customers, including both selling methods and physical distribution.

The different types of innovation, to which the different assumptions relate, can be pursued simultaneously in the same organization (provided it has the necessary resources), but they have to be clearly distinguished; confusion between them leads not just to misunderstanding but to expensive mistakes. Major changes in technology or markets are usually slow to make the transition from excitable reports in the media to the practical world where producers can make money out of them, politicians make capital out of them and consumers benefit from them. To pick examples more or less at random, carbon fibre technology took around thirty years from the time it was announced as tomorrow's engineering breakthrough to the time it had practical value; hovercraft have been hovering just as long, and still haven't made anybody any real money; news of medical breakthroughs abound, but any significant new drug will take at least twelve years to come to market.

If technological examples are regarded as a special case, take an opposite extreme like food consumption habits. Some thirty years ago, when Britain was finally emerging from wartime and post-war food rationing, I embarked on a lyrical report for an American processed food manufacturer on the revolution in the British diet. 'Before the war the typical diet was based on bread-and-spread, spuds and buns and lashings of sugar. But higher purchasing power, the development of convenience foods, the broadening influence of foreign travel have changed all that. Now the typical diet is based on', and then I checked the figures, 'whoops, sorry, bread-and-spread, spuds and buns and lashings of sugar.' Of course there are both technical and non-technical changes on the macro-scale, like the onward march of the computer and the progressive substitution of coffee for tea. But the progress is almost always slow, predictable and very expensive. There are many casualties along the road suffered by those who adopt a micro-thinking approach to macro-situations, rushing in too soon with too slender resources. The art is to get the timing right, the investment right and the build-up of resources right, not necessarily to be the first at table. But when you do arrive, you should have come for keeps.

The micro-marketing approach, seeking a quick competitive advantage by some innovatory step, designed to exploit an identified gap in the market or perceived customer need, is in many ways the reverse of this. In market sectors like fashion, travel, fast moving consumer goods and now fast moving financial services, your new 'customer propositions' probably will not have a long life. If they are successful your watchful competitors will hasten to imitate them, soon forcing profit margins down; if they fail, you will be left alone to give them a decent burial. Small companies, which are at a disadvantage in macro-marketing (because eventually – unless they grow very large very fast – they will be steamrollered by the giants) have an advantage in micro-sectors, because of their greater speed in decision-making and freedom from bureaucracy. They can be dug into the gap before the large competitor has gone through the tedious procedures involved in making up its corporate mind – and (if they are sufficiently realistic) out and on to the next project by the time the big battalions arrive. Things go wrong when the small companies get delusions of grandeur and think they can compete on equal terms with the large; or for that matter when the large companies apply the full weight of their macro-marketing systems to micro-projects.

Conventional thinking about innovation can also be damaging through excessive narrowness. Marketing textbooks and articles in marketing magazines and newspaper business sections tend to discuss innovation primarily in terms of new product development (the magazines unsurprisingly featuring the hopeful newcomers rather than the rejected flops). But thinking imaginatively about innovations that will at the same time benefit the customer and profit the company can often lead to the conclusion that changes in the delivery system or changes in the way employees are trained and motivated are more important than changes in the actual product or service.

The English clearing banks, for example, are currently involved not only in reviewing their range of services – which in the final analysis boil down to looking after the money customers deposit with them, lending them money and providing advice on money matters – but also in reviewing the way these services are 'delivered'; this involves the restructuring of branch networks (their 'delivery points') with increasing differentiation between business branches and personal branches, increasing specialization by bank managers and staff, and the progressive development of 'automated delivery points' outside their branches. All of this is more important in the long run than the new branded services that are being launched in bewildering numbers.

Equally the changes in selling and physical distribution methods made by food manufacturers in response to the fundamental post-war changes in the food distribution system have been more important in marketing terms than the new branded products that have been launched. Sales forces have been reorganized, with small numbers of negotiators capable of managing relationships with the large multiples replacing large armies of salesmen plodding around numberless independent outlets; physical distribution has been rationalized to meet the multiples' requirements through palletization, reorganized delivery schedules and so on; large sums of promotional money have been shifted from 'above-the-line' brand advertising to 'below-the-line' promotions, special offers and competitions focused on the point of sale. But washing powders remain washing powders, albeit with modifications in formulation and packaging; and baked beans are still baked beans, though now boasting progeny with different flavours, added sausages or whatever.

Organization

Organizing to release the innovative capacity that lurks in most people and most companies and to convert it into effective action is another problem with quite different solutions in large and small companies and in macro- and micro-marketing situations. To generalize, in defiance of my own principle that generalization is generally misleading, I would observe that small companies are good at producing new ideas, but bad at implementing them; while large companies, conversely, are good at implementing new ideas, if only they can be allowed to see the light of day. Yes, the contrary is also true; large companies can be highly innovative and small companies can founder through failure to notice that the world that gave them a living has changed and they must change with it. The art of innovation, where organization is concerned, is somehow to combine small-company flexibility with large-company follow-through.

The current fashion in Britain is to assert that innovative enterprise is the province of the small business, and to do everything possible to encourage more start-up businesses as a means of creating employment, getting Britain on the move again and so on. This is not good thinking. Overcoming the obstacles, mainly organizational, that inhibit innovation in large companies is probably easier than reducing the appalling death rate that afflicts small companies when they outgrow the strength of their initial idea.

The basic inhibitor of innovation in the large company is the fact that almost any change, even if it is ultimately for the better, is initially disruptive of efficient, profit-oriented management. What factory manager welcomes the news that a product change is required that will improve consumer acceptance, but necessitate retooling, retraining and probably arguments with the unions? What sales manager is pleased with instructions to close a number of favourite accounts that are no longer profitable, and attack virgin territory? How many profit-responsible divisional general managers submit without protest when they are told that their budgets must be cut to provide funds for diversification? How many chairmen look forward to telling the institutional investors that this year's profits will be down because of expenditure on projects that will pay off, if at all, in several years' time? While lip service may be paid to the importance of innovation, all the managerial pressures will give higher priority to milking today's business rather than investing in tomorrow's.

If the pressures can be resisted there are various organizational devices for ameliorating the poor relation status of the innovator, mostly depending on what American writers on management like to call 'champions' and 'godfathers'. The champion is the individual who is given the responsibility for investigating and solving or exploiting a defined marketing problem or opportunity, within agreed time and cost parameters; the godfather his patron in the corridors of power, who supports him when the going – as it usually does – gets hard. The organizational vehicle can be an inter-disciplinary task force, including marketing, R & D, production and financial specialists under the champion's command; or, more ambitiously, a separate venture capital division, operating as a cost centre rather than a profit centre. In either case, regular progress reviews by top management are essential, with godfatherly support to ensure that the project is not terminated prematurely while prospects are still good – but is terminated promptly if it runs out of road.

The venture capital division route was followed by the chief executive of an industrial gas company, concerned that the company was stuck in a profitable but hazardous rut, too exposed to changes in the fortunes or operating methods of its customers. He appointed to head the new division the then head of the company's R & D department – a rare bird among boffins in being as interested in the commercial applications of his developments as in their scientific sexiness. His brief was to seek diversification opportunities that had growth and profit potential in their own right and also made use of the company's core products; to develop them to the point where they were either commercially viable or clearly not going to make the grade; and then to kill off the latter and either transfer the former to one of the company's main operating divisions or hive it off as a separate business.

The new division did well in its role as mother ship for innovative new projects. A management team was built up with special skills and feeling for this type of activity. It had as expected its proportion of failed ventures, which were duly liquidated; and, as expected, it made an overall operating loss. But it launched successful ventures in such developing fields as fish farming and underwater welding, linked to the North Sea oil industry, and seemed to be setting the pattern for more ambitious innovations.

But then the chief executive godfather fell ill, retired and was succeeded by a new chieftain who, not unusually in such circumstances, took a diametrically opposite view of affairs from his predecessor. His view was that there was still a great deal of unexploited potential in the company's core business, particularly overseas, and that the venture division was a waste of time and management effort. Judging from the profit figures that followed (not to mention his own profit-sharing benefits) he was right. But there were those who wondered whether the liquidation of the venture division was not a case of flushing out the baby with the bathwater.

If the organizational problem of the big company is to accommodate infant projects, not allowing them to be crushed by the system while they are growing up, the small innovative company's problem is how to manage their successes as they grow bigger. Innovators tend to be anarchic, believing perhaps rightly that a degree of chaos stimulates original thinking. The trouble is that they are usually egotistical as well – they need to be to sustain their battle against the inertia of the establishment – and reluctant to recognize their own limitations. When the business gets too big for them to manage single handed, they refuse to let go.

People

So once again it comes back to people and to their capacity to manage themselves and their colleagues; to create productive relationships between the different talents and motives that must combine if bright ideas are to be captured and converted into profitable businesses; and above all to be humble about their ability to deliver a more acceptable product to customers than their competitors can offer, and patient in waiting for the pay-off.

The process of innovation can be compared with a funnel of widely varying dimensions – almost always wider and longer than seems likely in the first flush of inspiration – depending on the scale of the project. The mouth has to be wide enough to accommodate a great deal of relevant information, an adjustable vision of the future, alternative ideas for coping with the future (there are many ways of skinning a cat and most of them won't work) and a number of more or less awkward collaborators.

The last are invariably the greatest problem. Even on a small new project task force the chosen champion, probably a marketing man, has to establish a measure of creative harmony between R & D technicians, production people, sales people, advertising and design specialists and accountants – each with their different personalities, professional disciplines and ways of thinking. On a major techno- logical project it is more than likely, in today's internationalized markets, that the appointed godfather will have to seek help not only from bankers and university research departments but from overseas partners and government, with all the problems of communication and negotiation that this involves.

Over time the funnel will progressively narrow, as ideas are absorbed or discarded as unworkable in the light of further research and testing, collaborators serve their purpose and fade out, and the effort becomes more concentrated and focused. But the waiting time, not to mention the expenditure of money, can mount up frighteningly before the funnel's exit is reached – if it proves to have an exit; not infrequently it turns out to be a dead end. So persistence and indestructibility, combined with the capacity to sustain the support of collaborators and backers, have to be added to the qualities required of the successful innovator.

But in practice innovation need not be as formidable an affair as it sounds, once the conventional association between innovation, new products and advanced technology is set aside. The great leaps forward – from horse transport to the horseless carriage and the steam engine, from road and rail into the air, from the air into space – are of course a necessary part of the perilous progress of mankind. But their achievement requires a degree of power and vision – uncommon in contemporary politicians and managers – that is beyond the reach of the humble marketing man or the marketing-minded general manager. They can console themselves with the reflection that, for the practical purpose of giving greater satisfaction to customers, most innovation can be quite simple, short term and manageable – product improvements rather than revolutionary new products, improved delivery systems and after-sales service as well as product improvements, even just a more responsive relationship between supplier and customer.

Innovation on this more modest, but perhaps cumulatively more important, scale is a question less of inventive genius than of creating a culture and an organizational framework within which the natural inventiveness of many people can flourish and their creative ideas be nurtured (those of them that have a viable future) to the point where they are fit to face a competitive world. The well-known devices for generating new ideas, such as brainstorming sessions and quality circles, can be a useful starting point. But more important are the organizational arrangements for gently disposing of the ideas that definitely won't work and progressing those that have a chance (many of them also doomed to euthanasia at a later stage). Most important of all is the management-induced culture that accepts the need to allocate a proportion of the organization's resources to providing for change through innovation in good times as well as bad (most particularly in good times, since in bad times it is probably too late); a culture that involves everybody in the organization in the search for innovations, large or small, that can keep up with changing customer needs and so ensure a prosperous future for the organization.

There is a much loved anecdote about the little loved and exceedingly dictatorial American proprietor of a very successful international packaged goods company. He had arrived through practical experience, without benefit of business school, at a shortlist of basic business principles. Those of his employees who followed the rules were well rewarded; those who did not got short shrift. His periodic visits to his British subsidiaries were dreaded by those of his managers who had infringed such egalitarian rules as

'No private offices', 'Management and staff eat together', 'All grades clock in at the same (early) hour.'

A basic financial rule was that each business should earn an annual return on total assets of 20 per cent. So in one exceptionally prosperous year the imperial visitation was anticipated by local management not with dread but with great expectations of commendation and even tangible rewards. For the audited accounts showed a return on total assets of no less than 23 per cent. Alas for human hopes; instead of the approving smiles the meeting produced thunderous wrath. 'You're screwing somebody,' was the inelegant judgement, 'either it's me or it's the customers. If you're not giving the customers value for money, they'll make you pay for it; if you're not investing enough in the future of my business, I'll make you pay for it.'

It would greatly help the cause of organized innovation if the bankers and financial analysts who constantly hustle managements for higher and higher short-term profits would occasionally ask of the high flyers whose performance they commend: 'Is it the customers they are screwing or is it the shareholders, when they fail to invest in innovation?'

11 Has it a future?

The simple-minded marketing man, steeped in the belief that the road to riches is signposted 'Identify and satisfy consumer needs', is often puzzled by the financial news. For it seems that the quickest way to a fortune in a changing world is not through creating customer satisfaction but through finding and dismembering some rich but insufficiently agile company, to the evident dissatisfaction of those of its employees and customers who find themselves redundant.

Perhaps there is an element of envy as well as morality in the belief that financial predators, whose appetite grows with every new acquisition, do more harm than good and are rewarded beyond their deserts. That they do some good cannot be denied. Demolition contractors are as necessary as building contractors in the management of change; and there is no question that clearing a site is far faster and easier than the subsequent construction work. But whether sadly or smugly it has to be said that the marketer's skills belong in the building camp.

This applies with special force in the field of project evaluation, both internal innovatory projects of the kind discussed in the previous chapter, and external investments or acquisitions. The conventional financial expert looks at potential investments in terms of value for money, measured by profit trends and assets, before and after slimming treatment by the investor. The production expert or specialist in the relevant service industry is interested in technology, in whether the prospective acquisition or new venture employs, efficiently or otherwise, advanced rather than obsolescent technology. The manager or banker who fancies himself as a shrewd judge of people will have an opinion on whether those involved in the project are born winners or born losers and as a rule will investigate their previous track record. The marketer will ask first of all 'Has it a future?', and will answer the question in the light of what he knows or can find out about customer attitudes and needs, and his estimation of the new project's or prospective acquisition's ability to win present and future customer acceptance in the face of foreseeable competition.

It would be arrogant to claim that the marketer's view on the last criterion is the only one that really matters; a combination of skilled, if biased, judgements on all the relevant factors is better than any single view. It would be unrealistic also to deny that many investment decisions are based in practice on emotional or political considerations rather than objective judgement. Champions and godfathers fall in love with new product concepts and refuse to surrender them, despite irrefutable evidence that they should be abandoned. Politicians feel the need to proclaim a morale-building success and back a De Lorean project, despite the misgivings of their advisers; their successors, not they, will inherit the embarrassment. Acquisitive chairmen, faced with competition in a contested takeover, get the scent of battle in their nostrils and abandon reason for the sake of victory.

But even if 'Has it a future?' is not the only question to ask about a new venture, it is one that should not be overlooked in any but the most short-term wheeler-dealer enterprise. That it is so often ignored has to be counted a failure on the part of marketing, not so much in its technological aspects (for the techniques of marketing project evaluation are well developed) but in establishing a presence in the corridors of power.

Why did Imperial Group buy the Howard Johnson business in the US when anyone who knew anything about the American fast foods and leisure industry could have told them that its best days were behind it, and the future belonged to more modern chains like Macdonalds? Why the perpetual complaint that our national expenditure on research and development produces a lower commercial return year after year than comparable levels of expenditure by our competitors? Why, until recently, have the regional industrial development agencies spent so high a proportion of their funds on buying promised jobs that never materialized, because the new ventures on which they depended never earned a profit?

The simple explanation, I suppose, is that whoever makes the wrong decision in such cases probably has not paused to ask the right question before making it; and if the right question was asked has probably been too committed, for largely irrelevant reasons, to accept a negative answer. ('Whoever' in this case is a mysterious and usually collective pronoun; decisions as a rule seem to happen by default rather than being deliberately taken; it is difficult in retrospect, particularly when they have gone wrong, to determine precisely who was responsible.)

The right question from the long-term marketing viewpoint is whether there will be a profitable place for the project, as it comes to maturity, in the market at that (projected) time. This, of course, is a portmanteau question, incorporating a number of subquestions. What will be the pattern of customer demand in the target market segment in x years time? What will the competition look like? What will be the effect of currency fluctuations, government regulations and other environmental factors? Have the project's champions the capacity to deliver on their promises? Have they 'round two' staying power, to meet the counter-attacks from competitors that initial success invariably provokes?

Marketing has the techniques to answer some of the subquestions with a fair degree of reliability. Intelligent market research can usually determine which market segments are accessible, which of these have the best potential, what are their present characteristics, what future developments can be anticipated and how formidable the competition is likely to be. Research also can clarify financial and governmental factors when export or import substitution is involved, and forecast with some accuracy – barring revolutions or other accidents – any likely changes.

But the research and its interpretation need to be 'intelligent', in the sense that facts should be salted with judgement, not massaged into myopic clichés like 'growth market' or 'advanced technology'. Conventionally a growth market is regarded as far more attractive than a market sector that is static or in decline; but the latter may well offer a better opportunity to the ingenious newcomer than a growth market that is dominated by two or three powerful and progressive competitors. Advanced technology sounds modern and inviting; but it can be a disaster area for a newcomer with a single bright idea, but lacking the resources for the sustained R & D that is essential for long-term survival. The marketer needs balanced judgement even more than a battery of facts.

This is equally true when it comes to assessing the threat of competition. Factual data about competitors' market shares, growth rate, product acceptance and so on can be assembled by conventional market research means. It takes some experience and insight to forecast their likely reaction to a new threat – for example, whether their culture requires an immediate response, a period of observation and reflection, or lofty disdain for a small-scale incursion that may be profitable to you but would be trivial to them.

Subquestions about capacity to deliver on promises and staying power, also involving a large judgemental element, are not entirely within the marketer's province. The selling, promotional and distributive aspects of delivery are certainly marketing responsibilities; but whether the product will meet specifications, volume and cost targets are questions better answered by the relevant production experts. Similarly, the marketer can judge as well as the next man whether the project manager's or promoter's business plan has made adequate provision for round two and subsequent rounds; but the likely availability of the additional finance that will certainly be needed is better assessed by the financial experts. The essential points are that the questions should be asked and a holistic answer attempted; and, since judgement is such an important element in the answer, that if possible there should be alternatives to choose from. If put to it the marketer will undertake to provide a comprehensive answer. But he will feel more comfortable dealing with comparatives than with absolutes. When prediction is involved it is easier to say that this is the more promising of the available options than to certify any proposition as absolutely good or absolutely bad.

A homely example of this occurred when one of the Irish development agencies commissioned a firm of marketing consultants to evaluate a mushroom growing and processing project in search of government support. Reading between the lines of the brief – a habit that most consultants acquire – the appointed consultants were initially far from sanguine. The Emerald Isle is almost as addicted to dreams about mushrooms as to the little folk who dance at dawn among the shamrocks. Starting a mushroom business has the more tangible attraction because it requires relatively little capital, offering opportunities for subcontracting production to the small farmers who still abound there; and because of two ecologically favourable factors, a moist and mild climate and a plentiful supply of horse manure. What was often overlooked by optimistic entrepreneurs was that the country grows more mushrooms than it can eat and it is expensive to ship fresh mushrooms across the Irish Sea. The between-the-lines message of the brief was that the grant application had to be considered seriously because of the political influence wielded by the promoters, and the promise of new jobs (if all went well) in an area of high unemployment; but since a number of grant-aided mushroom projects had foundered in the past, a reasoned rejection would not be unwelcome.

To begin with the consultants were of a mind to oblige. It is always tempting to give clients the answer they are looking for; and while a positive recommendation invites disaster – for which the consultants, however blameless, will assuredly be blamed – a negative recommendation can never be put to the test. Moreover, there was nothing very new to the proposal, apart from a reference to the West German market for canned mushrooms as an alternative outlet to the British fresh mushroom market. Otherwise the same old story. Promoters with no previous experience in running a business. Collect manure. Make and impregnate compost. Use some in own mushroom sheds, sell rest (money in that) to subcontractors. Pick, pack or process and despatch.

But perhaps on second thoughts there was more to the West German reference than the customary obeisance to a notoriously large, though highly competitive and (in the case of mushrooms) static market. Other Irish entrepreneurs had cast longing eyes towards it, because of its unique appetite for canned mushrooms. Any producer of a highly perishable commodity can hardly fail to be attracted by the prospect of selling some of his output in a form which makes it possible to create a brand franchise and to carry stock, evening out short-term fluctuations in supply or demand. The problem was that the German supermarket and wholesale buyers already had an embarrassment of choice for their imported purchases between the French and Dutch producers just across their borders and producers in China, Korea and Taiwan whose low production costs compensated for long lines of communication and high tariff barriers. Irish agricultural produce had a good reputation among German consumers, partly because of good quality meat, dairy and other exports, partly because of the image, fostered by Tourist Board advertising, of a green and pleasant land, unpolluted by industry. But the supermarket buyers were not sentimentalists; product quality, price and strict adherence to delivery instructions, they made clear to the enquiring consultants, meant far more to them than any amount of imagery.

The significant point which emerged from a study of the market was that a Dutch mushroom canner, with whom the promoters had had preliminary talks about a possible sales agency arrangement, was highly regarded in the German grocery trade. But the firm was having some difficulty in supplying its customers with the required quality of product because its Dutch growers had been forced by high labour costs to change from handpicking to mechanical cropping. This might be a gap into which an Irish supplier could slip, especially if a firmer arrangement than a sales agency could be negotiated.

The owner of the canning firm was interested, when approached, in buying a minority interest in the Irish venture. It had the advantage from his viewpoint of giving him not only a certain supply of product whose quality he could help to assure but a potential source of personal income outside heavily taxed Holland. For the Irish promoters the partnership offered the benefit of a reliable German marketing arm to supplement the volatile fresh mushroom market in Britain; and of experienced help, including the loan of a production manager, in the commissioning of their cannery.

The marketing consultants, having helped to negotiate the partnership contract and persuaded the development agency that the project in its new form was worth backing, were not allowed to rest on their laurels. There were sceptical bankers to be convinced that a project based on a properly researched and thought-through plan was as creditworthy as a mortgageable but moribund asset. There were financial controls to be put in place, and a bright but inexperienced entrepreneur to be coached in the techniques of general management. Much of this activity was beyond the normal call of consultancy duty. But at the end of the day the consultants were able to sit back and reflect on a successful essay in project evaluation and the lessons that could be drawn from it. Two lessons, they thought, were important: first, that the key to any evaluation is very often the dog that didn't bark – the unconsidered possibility, which for better or worse makes this particular project different from others of the same ilk; second, that the amount of effort put into implementation can shift the odds significantly in favour of success.

New product development

But tilt the table as you may, the odds remain heavily weighted towards failure. Nowhere is this more true than in the field where marketing has the largest responsibility, that of organic new product development. Organic no longer in the sense of mushroom compost, but of developments related to one or other of the organization's main activities. The high mortality rate of such developments has tempted some marketing managers to keep their new projects under wraps until they come to fruition (or can be discreetly buried at dead of night) rather than exposing them to independent and possibly hostile criticism. This is shortsighted. Provided that enough new ideas are being poured into the mouth of the funnel described in the last chapter, it is more sensible to arrange regular management reviews of all projects from the conceptual stage onwards.

The most important reason for this is that it helps to secure the interest and support of specialist and line managers for the marginal projects whose success or failure is largely determined by the wholeheartedness of their implementation. A second reason is that the need to deal with regular bouts of criticism imposes a valuable discipline on the project managers, both in meeting time and cost deadlines and in ensuring that no important factors have been overlooked. A third reason is that an element of ruthlessness is needed in any long-term new product development programme – getting rid of the weaklings and blocking off the blind alleys in order to concentrate resources on the best prospects. New product champions become emotionally involved with their offspring and will cling to them after all reasonable hope of a profitable future is

gone; so an independent tribunal to pass sentence of death is
required.

But if it is to serve a constructive purpose, the trial has to be a fair
one, not settled as so often happens on the basis of prejudice or
ignorance. To bring this about it is necessary for the marketing
people involved to employ all their communications skills not in the
customary cause of persuasion, but rather in freeing the decision-
makers from preconceptions and enabling them to make an
objective choice. This requires a little more thought than the normal
procedures for organizing a meeting to ensure that it arrives
spontaneously at a prearranged result. In any preliminary papers
the purpose and background of the project under review need to be
spelled out, so that it is considered in context. Other ways of
achieving the original purpose need to be outlined, so that there are
more alternatives than just 'go ahead' or 'stop'. If the project is an
important one, the realistic assumption that half the people coming
to the meeting will not have read or understood the preliminary
papers needs to be covered by personal briefings of the key
decision-makers. And whether or not he personally chairs the
meeting itself, the marketing protagonist needs to make sure that it
is run in strict accordance with the principles laid down in William
Cooper's *Scenes from Metropolitan Life*:

> It's very important for people to have their say. The outcome of
> most meetings is obvious. But that doesn't mean meetings can
> be dispensed with. What people enjoy most is not the outcome,
> it's the way they get it.

In the end part of the art of organic project evaluation is
manoeuvring to make it more probable that the best of a range of
projects will survive a succession of trials by jury and only the worst
will be condemned before they face the even more perilous trial by
customer; an equally important part is to arrange matters so that
the survivors accumulate management support through the process
of internal trials, so enhancing the probability of success in the trial
that really counts.

Takeovers, mergers and megalomania

The failure of marketing to gain a decisive role at the summit of management (whether it be managing a business, a bank or a government) is particularly unfortunate when it comes to the macro-level of mergers, takeovers and the mania to build (often on insecure foundations) ever-larger international empires. There is nothing wrong with size in itself; in many international markets you need to be very big to survive. But size related to a rational assessment of what is needed to compete in the marketplace is one thing; size related to the compulsion to impress the investment analyst by non-stop growth in reported profits is quite another. The international conglomerate, now returning after being apparently discredited for ever in the 1960s, can make quick profits for a few promoters and investors but creates no wealth for the community. The fashion for purely financial deals, arranged and dominated by the money men, will presumably run its course and be discredited once again. It would happen faster if the decision-makers could be persuaded to think less about short-term financial gains, even about the economies of scale and the organizational synergy that so often turn out to be illusory, and to seek an objective answer in the marketplace to the question at the head of this chapter: 'Has it a future?'

'If only they would' is a pretty futile conclusion, when all the pressures on management argue for the short-term solution, a financial bird in the hand rather than a more productive but always uncertain future. There are things that marketing people can do – if they have any influence in the organizations they work for – to improve the quality of acquisition decision-making. The most obvious of these is to insist on an agreed strategy, defining the opportunity areas where the organization's special skills can be expected to count and specifying the criteria to be used in evaluating individual propositions. If taken seriously this does something to discourage the 'grass in the next field is greener' approach and the impulse to snap up an apparently good buy regardless of fit. If in addition the strategy is accompanied by a systematic search for suitable components in a thought-out design for commercial living five or ten years ahead, there is a reasonable chance of ending up with a larger but still manageable business.

Like any other theoretical approach, this will not always work. Propounding the relevant skills theory, I was stopped in my tracks by one amiable and cash-heavy client who responded: 'Special skills? Actually, old boy, we haven't got any.' On further investigation this turned out to be a very accurate statement.

There is also the key question of determination. One of the best statements of diversification strategy I've seen, worked out with the help of numerous consultants, was the proud possession of a firm in the declining but still very profitable tobacco business. But actual acquisitions and joint ventures over a long period were scanty and mostly ill-fated. Every failure had its own story, and there was one consistent thread. The firm's board were emotionally reluctant to accept a venture that did not promise the same handsome return as the core business. So any reasoned proposals were rejected for one of two Catch 22 reasons: either it was too big and therefore too risky, or it was too small and therefore not worth bothering about. The proposals that overcame this resistance were founded on political or emotional pressure rather than conformity with the reasoned strategy.

A market-led approach to growth by acquisition would be a great business, if it weren't for the people. Marketers are supposed to understand people. Perhaps we could do better in future.

12 Keeping the score

For anyone with a spark of romance, the marketing role of innovator, creator of new ideas and new products, apostle of improvement and change, is infinitely more alluring than that of general manager or accountant, saddled with the prosaic job of keeping the old machine on the road.

It has in fact turned the heads of many practitioners of the various aspects of marketing and even more of general managers inexperienced in its hard realities, who expect a dollop of promotional expertise to perform miracles. It is essential to remind such romantics that there's no such thing as a free lunch. With marketing (as with any other activity requiring inputs of time, money and effort for the sake of outputs of profit or other objectives achieved) it is important to count the cost and to have some mechanism for keeping the score. More frequently now than in the past, conscientious advertising agencies, recommending a staggering budget for a blockbusting commercial, insist that objectives should be specified and quantified and a proportion of the budget reserved for measuring results against these objectives. More frequently also, conscientious marketing consultants, invited to advise on marketing measures to revive a company's failing fortunes, will include a number of pointed questions about management information systems in an initial fact-finding foray. Sometimes problems are so urgent and obvious that an emergency operation is required; but as a rule it is foolish to embark on a long-term programme of change or even on some short-term innovation without a clear picture of where you are starting from and a reliable programme for measuring the incremental costs (or savings) and the benefits of the new initiatives. The Irishman's response to the motorist seeking directions, 'If I were you, I wouldn't start from here', will probably still apply; but at least if you know where 'here' is and have a reliable mileometer and petrol gauge, your chances of reaching your destination are improved.

It doesn't always improve the consultant's reputation, usually short lived, as miracle worker. Once upon a time (I recount it like a fairy tale, though it was surprisingly a fact) there was a branch manager of one of the large clearing banks who told a business client that he would renew his dodgy overdraft on just one condition – that he sought outside advice on his marketing. As beneficiary of this enlightened ultimatum I found the customary curate's egg situation of a small business that was good in parts. The range of kitchen utensils it offered was well-designed and well-made, though not particularly distinctive; the managing director, whose primary interest was in manufacturing, had a knack for picking up the bright ideas of competitors and finding an economical way of making something very similar. Distribution in the UK retail trade was reasonably good, though a quick shop check suggested a disturbing bias towards the more old-fashioned outlets. Some enterprising foreign sales trips (the managing director was an ardent traveller) had resulted in a larger flow of exports than would normally have been expected in a company of that size, particularly to the Near East and Eastern Europe. Because it was a small and very human company, there was a loyal but often mystified labour force. Management style was almost excessively hands-on. Not infrequently the sales manager could be found in the factory, packing an urgent order – and disrupting such control systems as existed.

The bad parts of the egg were that while everybody was driving with great determination down his chosen tramlines, the various activities often failed to connect; there were numerous internal personality clashes, the sales manager and the chief accountant being at odds about every conceivable point of policy or detail; and despite all the dedicated effort the company was trading at a loss. Worst of all nobody could identify the source of the loss, though there was general agreement – since there was no marketing manager to blame – that it must be a marketing problem.

'All right, let's agree it's a marketing problem', said the consultant medicine man, relying on the consultant's brief initial span of credibility, 'as long as you accept the broad definition of marketing as a management function. There's a lot of first aid we can do. We need to look at pricing policy to see if we can improve the operating margins. (Some of those export orders were clearly not worth having.) We need to rejig the salesmen's journey plans; they're calling on their old friends, not where the new business is to be had. No point in spending money on advertising, you can't afford enough to matter. It will do your reputation with customers more good (and probably reduce costs as well) to eliminate all those late deliveries and part shipments. But let's improve the packaging. It should cost you less and also get you better point-of-sale display.

That's just the first aid. If you want permanent good health, diagnosis must precede cure; and there must be continuous monitoring equipment. If you don't object I propose to spend as much time with the accountants, discussing cost accounting and management information requirements, as with the sales manager.' At which point credibility ran out and the managing director delivered himself of what as a professional marketing man I have treasured as one of the more memorable insults: 'I thought I had found a marketing adviser and it seems you're just another accountant.' A shattering blow to creative self-esteem.

Fortunately credibility was restored, as the first-aid measures began to work and the business returned to profit. Even more fortunate for the long term, the sales manager and the chief accountant were persuaded that after all they had interests in common; and it became possible to plan business and product development activities selectively, with a reasonably accurate measure of the financial implications of alternative courses. In short, the business became manageable.

A congenital reluctance to be mistaken for accountants has been the downfall of many well-endowed marketing men. A head of marketing who is carried away by the excitement of his own ideas for a glorious future and never counts the cost is well enough as one of the knights in a thinking chief executive's chess game, playing his allotted role, alongside the accountancy castles and the production bishops. But he can be a menace to his organization and ultimately to himself when he has full responsibility for major projects. Then he (or she) needs somehow to combine a vision of the future and a bold adventurousness with a cold calculation of the risk/reward ratio of alternative initiatives and a keen eye for escape roads (alias contingency plans) in case things go wrong.

The cautious, down-to-earth ingredients in this mix require an information and control system combining internal and external data sources which will enable a marketing manager, before committing himself to any major change in marketing tactics or organization, launching any major new product or attacking any new market segment, to obtain reliable answers to a battery of related questions such as:

1 How many potential customers (companies, stockists, people) are there in the target segment?
2 What needs do they have, within our range of expertise?
3 What share of their business do we have now?
4 How do our products compare for price, quality and reputation with our competitors' products?
5 What do our customers think of us in comparison with competitors?
6 How profitable is our existing business in this sector?
7 Are there differences in profitability between different sizes or types of customer within the sector?

Data sources are discussed in a later chapter. It is never easy to get a simple answer to a simple question, since sources have an irritating habit of disagreeing; and the cost of collecting information always has to be related to the practical use that is made of it. But by combining internal with external statistics, using underutilized sources like feedback from the sales force more systematically and adjusting suspect statistics with the aid of informed opinion, it should be possible to assemble figures that provide both a reasonable picture of the shape of things today and an adequate base for projections into the future.

From the factual data the marketing manager needs to construct a model (not necessarily a full-blown, computerized mathematical model but a concept of the way different market forces interact) from which to predict the effect of any proposed marketing action or of any anticipated changes in the market. It will be surprising if the predictions are wholly accurate, but that is not really the point. The purpose of quantified predictions of the outcome of innovatory projects, revolving around the relationship over time of revenue and cost (as well as any major side effects), is first to have a rational basis for choice between alternative investments of resources; and second to have a yardstick against which the progress of individual projects can be measured.

Even with a yardstick that turns out to be a metre rather than a yard long, measurement serves an invaluable purpose in keeping a project under control. If you look back over the history of almost any long-term marketing project, you will find that for better or worse its final shape was markedly different from the initial concept. Time scales change, as a rule lengthening rather than contracting. Levels both of revenue and cost are adjusted upwards or downwards – hopefully in step. Product specifications change as technical skills advance – or sometimes prove unequal to the original task. Expected customers fail to buy but, with luck, are replaced by others who had not been counted on.

Such changes are entirely acceptable if they represent a conscious reaction to new developments in a mobile environment; sticking inflexibly to a preconceived plan, when circumstances change, is as fast a road to disaster as any. What is unacceptable is unnoticed drift, with perhaps minor failures to meet deadlines, price targets, delivery schedules and other quantified objectives all being glossed over individually as a pity but not all that serious – and adding up to an unrecognizably distorted operation that would never have been acceptable if considered objectively in the first place. Regular measurement of progress on the main fronts, combined with serious investigation of the likely consequences of missed targets, provides an opportunity to pause and reflect before it is too late, considering whether to throw in additional resources in order to catch up, or to take an appropriate contingency plan off the shelf – or in some cases to abandon the mad gallop into the valley of death.

'If you look back over the history of a marketing project' is, I recognize, a hypothesis that discounts the predisposition of practical marketing people to look forward rather than back. When the story of a successful project is told, it is usually romanticized, with strokes of luck translated into acts of preternatural skill and the rough spots ironed out. When projects fail, marketing men like doctors would rather bury their mistakes than face a post-mortem. This is unfortunate. Much can be learned about the strengths and weaknesses of an organization, that will contribute to progressively improving performance, by an objective dissection of both successful and unsuccessful projects, more particularly the latter.

One company which recognized the potential benefit of a post-mortem, despite the possible embarrassment to the relatives of the deceased, expressed it very clearly in a brief to independent consultants who were required to investigate the history of an exceptionally calamitous new product launch and to 'establish the facts of what actually happened before and during the launch before they become myths; and from an analysis of the facts to derive any lessons which can be useful in planning and implementing other market development initiatives.' The story, because it demonstrated how easily people doing all the right things for the very best of reasons can produce the worst of results, might well be called:

The charge of the light brigade

Talent Ltd had been in business for over 200 years as the leading brewers in Erewhon. Their dark and creamy brew had established a dominant position as the national beverage, continuing to lead the market long after beer drinkers in other countries had transferred their affections to lagers and other lighter beers. There were defectors too in Erewhon, but their custom was not lost to the Talent organization which systematically acquired the main competitive breweries with their lighter brands, maintaining a total market share of around 90 per cent.

What worried the Talent management was first that the ale and lager brands did not bear the Talent name, making it seem that Talent was losing its grip on the domestic market, to the detriment of its export trade; and second that while the oldsters were addicted to the dark stuff, the new generation of drinkers did not care for it, calling it 'heavy, filling and soporific'. There was the nightmare prospect that within a generation the Talent group would be selling more beer under other people's names than under their own.

For a management proud of a historic reputation this was inadmissible. The decision was made to kill two birds with one stone by meeting the misguided taste of the younger generation for light beer (a taste shared, incidentally, by youth around the world and exacerbated by keep fit propaganda) and at the same time introducing the first major new product bearing the Talent name in two centuries. The single stone was to be a light version of the traditional Talent brew – light not in colour, which would have made it just another ale, but in specific gravity – that would appeal to young drinkers without seducing their seniors from the old original.

There were some members of senior management who were uneasy about the concept from the outset. Market segmentation is a useful theory, but in practice the segments are not as self-contained as pure theory would suggest. Some of the young share the tastes and habits of their elders and vice versa; and young and old do sometimes communicate with each other. A light dark beer is a clear enough concept to the expert, who distinguishes between the two meanings of light; but it is not easy to explain to the general public that lighter means weaker without implying that your new product is simply a watered-down version of the real thing. But Talent was staffed with loyal and highly motivated people. Despite individual misgivings a product development team in the brewery and a product development committee in the marketing department went to work with a will: the former seeking a product that would appeal to the young ale drinkers but differ in everything but appearance from the original dark stuff; the latter working with market research firms, advertising agents and designers to devise a name, a pack and an advertising campaign that would convince the target audience that here at last was their hearts' desire.

Considering that this was the first time they had tackled such a task in 200 years, both teams did a textbook job. The brewers produced test batch after test batch, subjecting them to the judgement of independent panels of light beer and dark beer drinkers, each comparing the new brew with the established market leader. The marketers drove the motivational researchers, designers and copywriters to distraction in pursuit of a promotional package that would at the same time impel the ale drinkers to switch to the new brand and reassure existing Talent drinkers that there was no need to change.

It cannot be said that either team was wholly successful. The brewers' best efforts did produce formulations that were better liked by ale drinkers than by Talent drinkers, but not very much liked by either; two out of three ale drinkers and five out of six Talent drinkers said after invigorating taste tests that, while they might give the new drink a try if it came on the market, they honestly preferred their customary tipple. The market researchers reported, after exhaustive investigations, that the most acceptable name for a lighter version of Talent would be Talent Light; and the advertising agents had the greatest difficulty in conveying in the same commercial that Talent Light was the greatest new development in 200 years but actually no greater than its long-established sister product.

But the more discouraging things looked, the more determined the project teams were to succeed. Warnings from the researchers that few new products succeed which do not win an absolute preference in taste over established competition were met with the wholly fallacious argument that one in three ale drinkers would add up to more than enough sales. The advertising agent with logical difficulties about positioning the new product was replaced by another, prepared to shout 'This is the greatest' and damn the consequences (the consequences, in the event, were widespread disappointment that the product didn't live up to the promise); and the heaviest weight of advertising ever seen in Erewhon was scheduled to compensate for any deficiencies in the product.

Such was the enthusiasm of the project teams that the periodic management reviews, held in accordance with the best product development procedures, became not objective reviews but hot-gospelling sales presentations at which faith was required to triumph over the unbelievers. In the end it became almost heretical for even senior managers to question whether market dominance, sales pressure, heavy advertising and gungho determination all combined could possibly fail to force a mediocre drink down the throats of a reluctant drinking public.

A final blow was administered on the eve of the product launch. The Erewhon publicans, who had long been in dispute with the Talent group about profit margins, dug in their heels. Certainly they would handle Talent Light, but only at a mark-up which would require them to sell it at 2p more than the regular Talent. There had been much debate, when the project was originally conceived, about the question of price; should the cost saving from the lower specific gravity be passed on to the consumer or added to the promotional budget? The view had prevailed that a lower price would imply lower quality and price parity had been agreed on. But a premium price for a weaker product was never thought of as a practical possibility. However, by this time blind faith was in the ascendant and the project was unstoppable.

The final outcome, everybody agreed in retrospect, was inevitable. The sales force performed prodigies in securing distribution and display for the new product; deliveries were on schedule; the advertising and accompanying PR created a considerable stir (in bibulous Erewhon this was after all a national event); and within two months half the beer drinking population had sampled Talent Light – as high a proportion incidentally among regular Talent drinkers as among the target ale and lager drinkers. But only 4 per cent of the samplers, according to follow-up research, intended to drink it regularly, and only 22 per cent thought they might drink it occasionally. Perhaps the waverers could have been converted if disappointment with the product's characteristics had not been reinforced by the mockery of traditional Talent drinkers, who declared that Talent Light was a cissy drink, fit only for novice drinkers – adding even more unkindly that the company was taking the novices for a ride by charging them more for a weaker drink. Sales in the first two months, when sampling was high, were not unsatisfactory, but descended steeply thereafter: at the end of eighteen months' strenuous efforts to retrieve the situation, the product was quietly withdrawn.

The main morals drawn by the consultant historians (mildly embarrassed by their own display of wisdom after the event) started with the need for quantified yardsticks that were taken seriously and for alternative approaches to the solution of a difficult problem. Keeping the score, as advocated in this chapter, is useful only when failure to meet targets results in corrective action, not simply a decision to move the goalposts; and corrective action is more readily taken when there are alternative routes to the same objective, so that management is not faced by a 'There is no alternative' ultimatum. In market development there is always an alternative – a different product, a different launch strategy, different forms of marketing innovation.

Other moralistic conclusions were that senior management should always be involved in the conceptual stages of major innovations, not presented with a *fait accompli* to accept or reject; that the claim 'research proves' should never be swallowed whole, for market research is seldom more than an approximation of the truth and can be wildly misinterpreted; that inexpensive market and consumer tests should whenever possible precede total commitment; and finally that a single spectacular failure should not deter management from further innovatory marketing projects. Being a realistic and resilient group, Talent's management was not deterred from further innovatory projects; but feet were kept much more firmly on the unforgiving ground of facts and figures.

13 What price training?

One of the first notions that will occur to the marketing impresario, as he contemplates the awesome task of making an organization more 'marketing oriented', is to send for the trainers. The idea that business education and training at all levels could make good the supposed deficiencies of British management, including marketing, was after all what motivated the establishment in the 1960s of the British business schools and the industrial training boards; and now that marketing is widely taught both by the business schools and polytechnics and by specialist training companies, we should be seeing the pay-off.

Perhaps management was not so black as it was painted in the first place; it has not been an easy job to manage in the face of fluctuating government attitudes towards business, variable rates of inflation, yo-yoing exchange rates, and social pressures for job creation and retention rather than productivity. Perhaps managers were too often unsympathetic to the idea of training, like the infuriated managing director who insisted in the early days of training board grants and levies that I help set up a training programme, training no matter whom in no matter what, as long as it averted the impertinence of a levy. But somehow or other a plethora of marketing professors appears not to have produced a notably higher standard of marketing performance.

Part of the problem is that the marketing academics have over-complicated matters. Even Theodore Levitt, the patron saint of marketing, has shown concern about current developments in the field. Writing from his eyrie in Harvard Business School, he has deplored in *The Marketing Imagination* (Free Press) the 'persistent tendency towards rigidity' inherent in the marketing concept, as in other business concepts and economic theories. While cleaving to the basic marketing principle that businesses should 'produce for customers what they clearly wanted, rather than merely trying to sell them what was being produced', he is clearly appalled at the creation in large American corporations of 'awesomely large and costly marketing departments complete with ponderously professional market researchers'. He is equally appalled that the impeccable principle of market segmentation has led in some cases to proliferating 'varieties of product and delivery preferences that push costs and prices ever upwards and increasingly out of customer and competitive reach'. The Japanese, he notes, have not done too badly in world markets by simply offering high-quality products at a low price on the massive scale that makes the low price possible.

It is not unusual for successful theorists to be dismayed by the elaborate edifice that others build on the simple principles that they have expounded. But Levitt's dismay illustrates one of the reasons why academic training in general marketing theory can be a two-edged weapon, when it comes to the practical problem of improving marketing performance in a particular organization. The educators very understandably are interested in advancing the frontiers of their technology and acquire merit in their peer group by so doing; the managers are interested in practical results and habitually count the cost of achieving them. There is a gap in comprehension between the two which it is sometimes difficult to bridge, despite the use of 'real life' case studies for marketing training purposes.

This is not to denigrate the business schools or question their educational value. Anyone heading for senior management is fortunate to go through the broadening experience and the opportunity to think through his personal business philosophy that they offer. What is questionable is whether the isolated action of sending key individuals on short or long external courses at even the best training establishments does anything to advance the cause of marketing orientation in the individual company. Only too often the report of returning course members is that it was a stimulating experience, interesting to meet a lot of chaps from other companies – all of whom seemed to have more interesting jobs – but really it was not very relevant to life in the old firm. Only too often their bosses greet the returning scholars with the message that it's business as usual now and any new-fangled ideas will be un-

welcome. Only too often, in the end, the only reward for the organization paying the course bill is a job vacancy.

This unhappy sequence of events can be guarded against by more careful preplanning, making sure that the selected trainees return to a new and challenging job and that the course curriculum is as relevant as possible to the requirements of the job. But when an organization is large enough to muster a quorum, it can be more cost-effective to organize a custom-built marketing indoctrination course for senior or middle management. This too has its hazards both for the company and for the prophet of marketing who rashly suggests that experienced managers may still have a thing or two to learn. Few companies share IBM's belief, handed down from the first Thomas Watson, that a company's annual investment in education, training and internal communications should increase at a rate that is greater than the company's rate of growth. In IBM, we are told, a first-line manager receives eighty hours of classroom training during his first year on the new job and at least forty hours a year thereafter; a total expenditure on education and training, estimated at $600 million in 1984, is accepted as a sound investment in the company's future. IBM can be regarded as a special case, because of its size and situation in an industry of constantly changing technology. But no organization is immune to change in customer needs and attitudes, in the characteristics of the products required to satisfy them, and in methods of linking the two.

Yet in all too many companies and individual managers there is resistance to the idea that the learning process should not cease when school or college education is over but go on for the rest of life; the invitation to go back to school is regarded as an insult, and time spent away from the job is looked on as money lost to the company. Both the course organizer and its sponsor are at risk, if the course is not at the same time stimulating and clearly relevant to the company's business. The sad glissade when these conditions are not satisfied will be familiar to anyone who has organized or participated in these events. The late arrival of individuals who want to make it clear that they are really too busy to tear themselves away from their desks; the emergency telephone calls from secretaries; the excessive patronage of the bar; the ill-concealed impatience with any academics who may have been invited to dispense wisdom; the stiff upper lips of managers whose loyalty forbids them to reason why, but who still visibly wonder why they are there; and, at the end of the day, confirmation of the lurking suspicion that marketing (like democracy) is a fine catchword but nothing to do with the practicalities of running a business – and, more to the point, a marketing department is a luxury that the company can ill afford.

There are ways of avoiding such a wholly negative outcome. It helps if whoever organizes the course curriculum spends a substantial amount of time before the event chatting with prospective course members and their bosses, to establish their real life problems and level of marketing sophistication, so that the course really is custom-built and not a standard chassis with a few additional trimmings. It helps if the marketing theory element – 'the difference between marketing and selling' and so on – is kept to a minimum; the gap between theory and practice is too wide for most people to leap. It helps if the course is highly participative, so that members are challenged and involved, instead of sitting with cynical smiles on their faces. It helps if any case studies are built, if not around specific company problems, at least around a recognizably similar organization. It helps if a respected member of senior management can be induced to give the course his seal of approval by his presence and his active participation.

But however successful the five days (which seems to be the standard duration of such courses) it is unrealistic to expect that there will be significant differences in the behaviour and attitudes of course members after treatment. A single course by itself can be no more than an encouraging signal by management that it has some confidence in the value of marketing. For training to make a real contribution towards changing a company's orientation in a more marketing-led direction, a much more serious long-term programme is needed; and it needs to be combined with other organizational and motivational changes.

One medium-sized company in the financial services industry, which had tried the five-day conversion treatment without noticeable effect, made a fresh attempt at solving the problem of cost-effective marketing training when a new head of marketing had found his feet and been joined by a more progressive personnel manager. The attempt followed an intensive investigation into the needs and attitudes of customers and potential customers, the activities of competitors and the more predictable market trends; and management agreement on the marketing strategy that the company was best equipped to follow. So it was possible to develop a marketing and sales training programme within a clearly defined concept of the types of customer the company would be doing business with, the propositions that would be put to them, the product knowledge and presentation skills that would be needed to persuade customers that the propositions were superior to those of competitors, the back-up services required to ensure that promises were not broken, and the combination of efficiency, good manners and creative ingenuity that would eventually convert promising acquaintances into contented long-term relationships.

From this a manpower budget and skills matrix was constructed (all of this sounds highly theoretical, but the way it actually happened was much less methodical), spelling out the number of people – some of them in place, some to be found – needed to play the different marketing, sales and back-up roles; and the ideal combination of knowledge, skills and attitude for each role. Next, in logical though not in historical order, came the design of training modules to fit into the various slots in the matrix, under such headings as presentation skills, communications skills (writing a clear and simple report was as rare a skill in this as in most other companies), interpreting market information, identifying customer needs, product knowledge, and the general understanding of the company's policies and culture that can be rather loosely aggregated under the heading of marketing attitude.

Next came the question of how each module could best be constructed. Some could be incorporated in the company's existing training programme, like the much neglected detail of persuading secretaries and switchboard operators to sound as if they welcomed callers and wanted to be helpful, instead of transferring them to an extension that never answers or promising a return call that never comes; good manners are seldom listed in the more high-falutin definitions of good marketing, but in a service business they can be as important as the right price. Other modules, like product knowledge, required the participation as part-time trainers of specialists from within the company. This had the advantage of building some rapport between the specialists and the customer service executives who would rely on them for day-to-day back-up. But there were difficulties not just in persuading the specialists to spare the time away from their desks but in helping them to organize sessions that demystified their subjects, concentrating on communicating the customer benefits rather than the technicalities.

Other modules again were better handled, it was felt, by independent experts, who combined didactic skills that the company's own executives could not match with an up-to-date knowledge of the marketing and selling methods used in other companies or other industries. These modules covered subjects like presentation and communications skills – identifying customer needs, making face-to-face or written proposals, writing succinct reports – where general principles are as important as the particular message. It was an advantage that some of the training companies considered – the personnel and marketing departments sent guinea-pigs on their open courses to determine which were best at matching performance to the promise of their brochures – were equipped to produce interactive and audiovisual learning pro- grammes which client companies could retain and use for refresher training or indoctrination of individuals, when numbers of trainees were too small to justify a full-blown course. None of the selling techniques advanced by the various training companies would be unfamiliar to any old-school salesman (one indeed recommended 'a special concept developed by Mark Twain', whom few admirers of *Huckleberry Finn* would associate with sophisticated modern salesmanship); but all were skilled at analysing the components of what has been traditionally an instinctive skill, breaking them down into bite-size portions that the less skilled could assimilate.

Inevitably, in the course of the lengthy discussions that led to the development of the training programme, the objection was raised that this was not a marketing training programme but a multilevel programme in basic administration and selling. What had become of marketing technology, product development, market research, planning and the rest? What was being done to tackle the problem of individual attitudes and corporate culture, shifting both along the well-worn track from production orientation to customer orientation? The rebuttal was wholly pragmatic. First of all, the training programme was designed to be continuous, year-in and year-out, and would be progressively changed and improved in the light of experience. But it had to be established as cost-effective in the eyes of a sceptical management (who did not yet share the IBM philosophy that it pays off in the long run to allocate 15 per cent on average of every executive's time to appropriate forms of training). For this purpose it was sensible to begin with the aspects of marketing most immediately linked to tangible results, like improved selling and customer service. More sophisticated aspects of marketing could follow.

Second, the specialists in the marketing department would be required as part of their responsibilities to act as interpreters between the outside providers of market information, advertising and promotional material and other marketing services, and the users within the company. They would be sent on appropriate external courses to keep their expertise up-to-date, as well as participating in the internal courses on selling and presentation skills. To the extent that they became good communicators, the need for detailed understanding of marketing techniques on the part of users would be obviated.

The question of marketing attitudes and culture was the subject of more anxious debate. Rightly or wrongly it was concluded that training can make only a minor contribution to changing attitudes. It must, of course, be in tune with the prevailing culture – or its more progressive features in situations, not uncommon in the prevailing climate of mergers and takeovers, where there are two warring factions; visiting trainers accordingly were asked to spend some time acclimatizing themselves by meeting key individuals at various levels in the organization before dispensing wisdom. The conventional sessions on 'the kind of company we are' need to be included in indoctrination courses. But it is what happens on the job, the kind of company it really is, that determines attitudes, not the pieties and motherhoods of a training course. In the end it was agreed that the development of more marketing-oriented attitudes down the line must be a function of day-to-day management, and a senior management seminar (at which the head of marketing, having helped to set the scene, kept a conscientiously low profile) was organized to discuss ways and means.

The seminar offered an opportunity to co-ordinate off-the-job training with a more active management involvement in the improvement of marketing performance and understanding on the job. On a formal level the clause about responsibility for training subordinates – included along with profitability, the maintenance of high operating standards and the kitchen stove in the job specifications of all departmental managers – was reaffirmed and made more specific; the selection of individuals to attend courses, the preliminary briefing and the debriefing were made more systematic; and more weight was given in the performance appraisal system to the business development contributions of junior management and support staff. On a less formal level some progress was made towards establishing the principle that every department and departmental manager had a contribution to make to the cause of better marketing. As the marketing manager remarked, good resolutions do not make a millenium; but at least there would be a foundation of better understanding to build on.

Because training in general and marketing training in particular is so badly needed in British management, it would be pleasant to conclude this anecdote with a happy ending. 'And after the first two years the company's rating with customers and its market share improved by x per cent – an improvement that could only be

attributed to the improved marketing performance of its people.'
The difficulty with this is that the story has not ended, will never end
in fact if the principle is accepted that training is an unending
process; and that the interactive nature of marketing, with product
formulation, price, promotion, selling and customer service all
contributing to the end result, makes it difficult to isolate any one
factor as crucial. That training will make a cost-effective contribution must to some extent be an act of faith.

But faith is more likely to be justified if marketing trainers learn
from the mistakes of the past, avoiding in particular the arrogant
assumption that force-feeding sceptical managers with the pure
milk of marketing theory will achieve any useful result; and being
very cautious about exposing the young and innocent to the kind of
case study work which starts with the assumption that 'You are the
managing director of the XYZ Company' when their prospects of
being managing director of anything within the next twenty years
are minimal. Training needs to be relevant and actionable, if it is to
be cost-effective.

It is an article of marketing faith that all rules should be given due
consideration and then broken; otherwise change and progress will
be impossible. Nevertheless the marketing manager or adviser,
seeking to accelerate change through training, should consider the
following few practical training rules rather carefully before
breaking them. Failure to observe them has caused not a few
catastrophes.

1 Look on marketing training as a continuous, long-term,
   evolving process, not confined to the classroom. A marketing
   indoctrination course in isolation is a waste of time and money.
2 Analyse 'marketing' into skill, knowledge and behavioural
   modules. Infiltrate appropriate modules, if possible, into
   existing in-house courses.
3 Segment trainees, including those not in specifically marketing
   jobs, relating training modules to the requirements of the
   individual job.
4 Start with the practical rather than the theoretical aspects of
   marketing. Communication skills, whether face-to-face,
   written or telephone, negotiating skills, product knowledge
   with the emphasis on customer benefits, identifying customer

needs and selling opportunities, and common-or-garden (not so common actually) good manners, all salted with a proper concern for the bottom line, will do to start with.

5   Understand the culture of the organization. Over time you may be able to redirect it, if you can get the organizational power brokers on your side; but training that directly opposes it will get nowhere.

6   Keep the main weight of the training in-house, with whatever outside assistance is needed. Don't forget programmed learning systems for individual or refresher training sessions.

7   Time individual training exposure, when possible, to coincide with a change of job, promotion or other occasion requiring new patterns of behaviour.

8   Combine off-the-job with on-the-job training.

9   Use internal marketing communications and events like new product launches as a means of reinforcing the marketing training message.

10   Make sure that the marketing performance required at each level in the organization is featured in the organization's performance evaluation or management by objectives systems.

11   Above all, secure the continuing support of senior management and the personnel department, providing as much evidence as possible that marketing training produces practical results. It's easy to become a voice crying in the wilderness when training is the issue; there are other more important battles for marketing to fight in the management of change.

Part Three

A Relevant Professionalism

In the first two parts of this book I have argued that marketing has disappointed its admirers over its short history as a would-be management science, partly through too narrow a view of its function. In some organizations it is true that marketing men have won seats at the high table of corporate management and it has been accepted that an awareness of marketing principles must permeate the whole corporate body; but in only too many the marketers are simply those overpaid chaps who look after the advertising and market research.

Marketing practitioners and teachers have compounded this narrow view by an undue concentration on techniques rather than practicalities, implying that qualified marketers can become members of an exclusive priestly caste, speaking a different language from common mortals. Certainly there are special skills involved in market research, marketing communications, product development and so on; a high level of professionalism in these activities is obligatory. But professionalism is wasted if it is not relevant to the objectives of the organization within which it is practised – and if its end products are not communicated in understandable terms to other members of the organization whose co-operation in marketing enterprises is essential.

In this third part I discuss the key responsibilities of marketing professionals towards the organizations that employ them; and consider some of the reasons why growing professionalism has not always resulted in an equivalent contribution to the success of the organization concerned.

14 Guarding the brand name

Investment advisers who assess companies on the basis of the latest year's profits, bankers who secure loans on tangible assets, miss a vital point that Iago (almost) got right many years ago:

> Who steals my purse, steals trash; 'tis something, nothing;
> 'Twas mine, 'tis his and has been slave to thousands;
> But he that filches from me my brand name
> Robs me of that which not enriches him,
> And makes me poor indeed.

A brand name (or good name, as Iago called it in his old-fashioned Venetian way) can be attached to a company's product, to the company itself or to a non-commercial organization, even a country. It is a precious possession, more valuable and potentially more durable than a product formulation which may need to be modified, or a factory which will certainly need to be modernized, or a management team that will wear out and need to be replaced. And it is a primary responsibility of the relevantly professional marketer to safeguard it during his period in office and pass it on, enhanced and if necessary transmogrified, to his successors.

That marketers have often failed to discharge this responsibility is partly due to a long-standing confusion between the brand and product, and partly to a once popular and highly dangerous marketing theory, the product life cycle. According to this theory every product (or brand), like every mammal, has a predestined life span with clearly defined stages. The product, as well as the mammal, has a period of infancy, when it is a charge on its parents and requires considerable investment of effort and money to equip it for survival in a competitive world. If the product is successful, says the theory, it soon moves into a second stage of rapid growth, during which with luck it will start to earn profits. There follows a third stage of maturity, when sales level out and competition makes profits harder to earn. Finally comes the fourth stage, of inevitable decline, when the responsible marketing manager has to decide whether to continue the struggle for survival; to milk the product for such profit as may be left in it; or to put it painlessly to death (never easy, since there is always at least a handful of addicted customers).

The theory, though superficially a truism, is dangerous in a practical way because it is very hard to be certain what stage a given product has reached. For instance a product that appears to be on its last legs may gain a new lease of life through the discovery of a new use or group of users, if a theory-driven marketer has not already written if off. The psychological effect of accepting what may well be premature demise as inevitable can be even more serious when product and brand are confused. A manufactured product can soon become obsolete in an age of rapidly advancing technology. But the product concept, for which the brand name stands, can live on. Ford, the model T vehicle, became a museum piece many years ago. But Ford, the concept of reliable, value-for-money transportation, lives on.

An even more homely example is the washing powder Persil. In the late 1940s, when soap was still rationed, Persil, then the market leader and a soap-based product, was clearly doomed to decline in the eyes of the bright young marketers (me included) who were concerned with the introduction of the synthetic detergents like Tide and Daz. More efficient (particularly in hard water) and unrationed, the modern synthetics could not possibly fail to unseat poor old-fashioned Persil.

In the late 1980s Persil, no longer soap-based, is still the market leader. It is by no means the same product – or even a single product having evolved over the years in step with advancing detergent technology and split into different formulations for different applications. It is not used in the same way, thanks to the advent of fully automatic washing machines. Even its users are not the same, a new generation of housewives, househusbands and single parents having taken over from the obsessive housewife of the 1940s (if she ever really existed) determined to demonstrate affection by keeping her children's shirts whiter than white. Even the pack and the advertising are different in detail if not in spirit.

Yet it remains the same old reliable brand, no different essentially from its competitors, but the one that most users feel comfortable with, and the one consequently that commands the most shelf space in the supermarkets and other stores. A trivial example perhaps (the world would not become noticeably more unpleasant if Persil disappeared from its face) but in its way a shining example of the micro-marketing function of guarding the brand name.

It could be argued that the marketing factors which kept the Persil persona ahead of the competition long after the original Persil product had become obsolete are not widely applicable. Advertising by an agency that believed very strongly in maintaining an emotional as well as a logical relationship with customers was a very important factor, supported by motivational research probing such psychographic questions as: 'If Persil were a person, what would he or she be like?' Not all brands or all companies (when the company's name is effectively the brand name) are active in markets where heavy advertising is effective or affordable. Washing powders represent an answer to the well-nigh universal demand for personal cleanliness (those who eschew cleanliness tend to be short of purchasing power, and so unattractive commercially as well as odorously); and it is an answer that has yet to be superseded by radical advances in technology, such as dirt removal by ultrasonic beams. Some product categories get superseded in this way, though seldom so fast that the owner of the brand name, if sufficiently agile, could not diversify into a more technologically advanced answer to the same need; a Chinese abacus manufacturer could still have time to transfer his brand name to personal computers. Persil was fortunate also in the strength of its sales force and in the growing dominance of the retail grocery chains which favoured the nationally advertised brand leaders and made it harder for new brands to break into the market.

But the principle remains good that a brand name, whether attached to a product, a company, or a country, is a precious possession, when it stands for something that gives confidence to customers. It may be efficiency, reliability, value for money, good service, honesty, humanity or a combination of all these qualities. It has to be genuine; no weight of advertising claims on behalf of the caring bank or the reliable car, no amount of PR expenditure or sponsorship of good causes will improve the brand image, if the bank manager is conspicuously uncaring and the car keeps breaking down. It usually takes a long time to establish. It needs constant care and attention. It can never be perfect or universally accepted; even perfection has its detractors, witness Aristides the Just who was just so perfect that the Athenians could not endure him and voted for his exile. Marketing should take the lead in guarding it, and should take the blame if it is lost. Admittedly the reasons why the brand is damaged or destroyed are often complex and outside the narrowly defined control of a marketing manager, but it must be his responsibility to see the whole picture of what is happening and initiate remedial action before it is too late.

Take as an example the history of the rise and fall of the Danish national brand as the dominant brand of bacon in the UK. It could be called:

Self-destruct: a tragedy in three acts

Act I: Creating a brand

Before the 1939–45 war, Danish bacon was simply bacon that came from Denmark. It was sold through a number of agents in the UK, each strong in a given area; and it had the considerable competitive advantage of consistent quality. English, Irish or Dutch bacon at its best could be at least as good; but at its worst it was very much worse.

This quality advantage was due, first of all, to the fact that the British market was of primary importance to the Danish farmers and the co-operative factories that processed their bacon pigs for the British market – which absorbed a great deal more bacon than was consumed on the domestic market and received priority treatment. The Landrace brand of bacon pig was developed to meet the needs of the British market. A streamlined animal, not so fat as the general purpose pig (which is more suitable than the Landrace for consumption as pork), it had the dual advantage of meeting the consumer taste for lean rashers and being easier for the butcher to cut into saleable portions. This second feature was important at a time when bacon was sold mainly in sides to be finally cut up in one or other of the great number of independent grocers that flourished at that time. Most important of all was the willingness of all the co-operative bacon factories, with one or two exceptions, to sell their bacon through a single marketing organization and conform to common quality control standards.

The pre-war and immediate post-war period was, of course, the golden age of the Great British Breakfast, when bacon and eggs was the ideal of all who could afford it, and the muesli phenomenon was still confined to eccentric Swiss clinics. Danish bacon became the central feature of the British breakfast, accounting for nearly half of the total national consumption. Its reputation was such that retailers found it worthwhile to identify rashers and joints as Danish in their display cabinets; and the price of bacon from all other sources, including English, was set on the London Provision Exchange in terms of a discounted figure below that posted by the Danes and their agents.

Act II: Changing market, changing faces

In the first two post-war decades this position of strength was consolidated by effective marketing. An office was set up in London to represent the interests of the Danish agricultural producers, initially through an information service and other PR activities, and subsequently through advertising, point-of-sale merchandising and a technical advisory service for the distributive trade. The advertising had the advantage over the sporadic efforts of competitors that it ran consistently, year-in and year-out; and that it was promoting a product that actually was better than its competitors. It was fortunate that at the time the London office and its parent organization in Denmark were both run by strong men, who were able to persuade the Danish farmers that it was in their long-term interest to put the customers first (remote as they were) and accept a degree of discipline to that end.

But then the market began to change, starting with the consumer revolution in the home. As more and more wives went out to work and breakfast time became a pandemonium of parents and children all rushing to go their separate ways, the tradition of stalwart mum dispensing hot meals from the hot cook stove began to fade; and the lost breakfast rashers had to be replaced by snacks, joints and other less convincing substitutes. More seriously the character of the grocery trade was revolutionized by the advent of the self-service supermarket and the shift of trade from small independent stores, served by wholesalers, to regional and national multiples, buying direct and with enough purchasing power to dictate their own terms to all but the strongest suppliers.

A third agent of change was the technological development of vacuum packing bacon rashers, cuts and joints in film, giving them a longer shelf life and making obsolete the traditional bacon hand who could actually cut up a side of bacon. This was not a happy development for the Danish producers. Their technical advisory service lost much of its point when bacon became just another prepacked commodity; and the advantage of a specially bred lean rasher was largely lost when the fattest bacon could be trimmed to look lean before being vacuum packed.

The Danish producers did their best to adjust to the changing situation. Like most market changes involving a massive shift in consumer habits, it did not happen overnight; it took a generation for family shoppers to adjust to the different taste of prepacked rashers and the pleasures of queuing at the supermarket check-out. This allowed time to build a Danish bacon packing factory in Norfolk, at the time the largest and most modern in Europe, and to establish an understanding with the multiple grocery buyers that they would continue to buy their Danish bacon from the central marketing organization at a fixed price, rather than negotiate direct with the individual factories in Denmark and play one off against the other. Any price concessions took the form of special offers, linked to in-store promotions, rather than overt discounts.

Act III: Dissolution

As the multiples got stronger and rival producers stepped up both their product quality and their marketing effort, the situation became increasingly unstable. The Maginot line was held by two strong men: one running the marketing organization in Denmark and persuading the restive farmers and factory managers to accept the long-term view, 'United we stand, divided we fall', against all the temptations of opportunism; the other running the promotional organization in London and insisting on the importance of consistently strong advertising, merchandising and PR, despite a fluctuating market and the anguish of the farmers, who complained that the money would be better spent on feeding their pigs or even their families. They were supported in their obstinacy by the loyalty of the British consumers, who persisted in their belief that Danish bacon – and, by association, other Danish products – were good enough to merit a premium price; and of the main agents, whose job of receiving orders from the multiples and wholesalers (sometimes themselves) and transmitting them to Denmark looked like a soft option but involved a level of market knowledge that was not fully appreciated by the Danes.

But then everything started to fall apart. The two strong men retired, having failed, as is the common weakness of their kind, to provide for a strong succession. The largest of the main agents, which was also an important wholesaler partly Danish owned, got into financial trouble and was taken over by the Danish marketing organization. The bacon packing factory had increasing difficulty in obtaining the best quality of bacon from the Danish factories, as the latter began to divert their best product to other markets like Japan, which in the short run looked more profitable. The new management running the UK marketing organization decided to save money by dispensing with the services of the main agents and setting up their own national sales force, creating an unexpected amount of dislocation and ill will in the process. The key wholesaler, despite its Danish name and ownership, sought salvation from its financial problems by dealing in Dutch and German as well as Danish bacon. Worst of all, the co-operative bacon factories in Denmark – seduced on the one hand by the erratic attractions of markets outside the UK and on the other by the blandishments of the large British multiples, anxious to buy the best quality bacon direct for sale under their own labels, and lacking in strong leadership – began one by one to secede from the central marketing organization.

On the surface, as the British consumer sees it, the situation is not greatly changed. Danish bacon still has a fine reputation since reputations earned over many years are not lost overnight. It still accounts for a high proportion of UK bacon sales, though not all the best bacon comes to Britain, and not all of the best that does come is sold through the central marketing organization. Danish bacon is still advertised – though with a dwindling sales volume on which to base it, the weight of advertising is bound to fall. But the producers, though they may not recognize it back on the farm, have lost an invaluable asset – the control of a dominant national brand name. The brand has been atomized, with control passing to the multiples and other major UK concerns, together with the few Danish factories, like Tulip, promoting their own brands in the UK. While the Danish origin will be featured as long as it impresses the consumer, the main reputation will be transferred progressively to the multiple or factory brand. Their marketers will control the quality and the price, setting both at the level most appropriate to the individual organization; and if in the long run it suits their book to replace the contents of their packs or cool cabinets with bacon from some source other than Denmark, they will be free to do so.

I could be accused of unfairness in calling this a marketing failure. After all, there was nothing wrong with the technical side of the Danish bacon marketing operation. The very best market research was used, throughout the rise and fall of the 'brand', to track market shares and consumer attitudes. The advertising was of consistently high quality, switching its emphasis from rashers to joints and from breakfast to other meals as consumer habits changed. With the very imaginative PR activity it did a great deal to sustain the whole bacon market, in the absence of consistent competition from other producers. The point-of-sale merchandising and the technical advisory service, if not faultless in execution, were of a standard that few manufacturers' marketing organizations at the time were able to match. Did the root causes of the brand's decline not lie in a radically changing marketplace, in failure of people with the power of decision to take the right decisions to cope with the changes, and in failure to concentrate on the key long-term priorities – all exacerbated by the split of responsibility between two countries?

Admitted. This was a macro-marketing and not a micro-marketing failure. Given human fallibility, it would have been difficult to avoid. But it was not inevitable; and a far-sighted strategic marketing approach that paid as much attention to the importance of internal communications and persuasion as to external customer relations could have bridged the gap between the old market and the new. The professional marketers' problem in such cases is not so much to see what needs to be done, but to persuade the politicians, the financiers and the careerists who so often occupy the seats of power that it is in their interest to protect the brand that supports them at whatever short-term cost to themselves.

The secrets of long life for a successful brand are no secret at all. They are: sensitivity to the changing needs and attitudes of customers and of distributors or other intermediaries; consistently high standards of service; consistent advertising and promotion; adjustment to new technology in distribution and communications as well as production; and a product that changes imperceptibly in substance and presentation as the market and technology advance, while preserving the respect and affection of its customers. The decline and fall of brands, whether attached to manufactured products, services, organizations or countries, is usually due to a loss of vitality not in themselves but in the people who run them. The marketer who aims for a fundamental success has to start with the people – convincing those on his own side before he tackles the enemy.

15 Keeping in touch

The marketing responsibility for safeguarding the brand name requires a sensitive understanding of the customer, the competitor and the marketplace in all their manifestations. Market research is a valuable tool for keeping in touch with all three. *Ergo*, technically sound market research should be above criticism by even the grouchiest of marketing critics. The logic, if not irrefutable, is plausible and is supported by the fact that research is the acceptable face of marketing for those who reject its more ambitious claims.

I first learned about this equivocal acceptance long ago when I was last to bat at an advertising agency presentation to a notoriously ogrish client. After my far more eloquent colleagues had held forth to a markedly unreceptive audience about marketing strategy, creative execution and the rest of it, I said timidly that I would like to say a few words about the role of market research. The ogre smiled.

'Ah, market research, I have a soft spot for that.'

This gave me courage to enlarge on the agency's belief in the importance of research as a basis for consumer-oriented promotional strategy and as a check on the effectiveness of the creative performance. I did not go down well.

'Young man, you must have misunderstood me. When I said that I had a soft spot for research, I did not mean that I take it seriously. I just enjoy reading it and being told what I already know.'

'But sir, supposing it doesn't confirm your own prejudices, excuse me, experience?'

'Well then I tell the researchers to go away and do it again – and to get it right this time.'

At the time I was righteously indignant at the ogre's cavalier attitude to scientific methods. How dare he question the infallibility, within an acceptable margin of error, of figures resulting from a meticulously constructed and pretested questionnaire, submitted to a random (well, almost random) sample.

Forty years later I have come very close to sharing his viewpoint. The results of even the best sample surveys are not infallible, but simply an approximation to the facts at a particular time (already in the past). They can provide a useful piece of evidence, to be weighed with other evidence before making a decision. But they should not be accepted uncritically as the sole evidence justifying an arguable course of action. Nor should the situation they indicate be regarded as immutable. 'That is what our customers (or constituents) think at the moment; now what do we do to change their minds?' can be a more constructive reaction than acceptance of the inevitable.

So far as techniques go, commercial market research is a branch of marketing that the profession can be modestly proud of, as a practical amalgamation of borrowings from more than one academic field. Applying the statistician's sampling theory (which tells us that eventually red and black will come out even on the baccarat table, if we don't go bust waiting) to surveys of public opinion and behaviour was an imaginative development scarcely fifty years old. It took time to convince people that a couple of thousand representative individuals could speak for a population of 50 million or 250 million and answer at least the simpler questions in much the same way as the total population would. Doctor Gallup's famous dialogue with the sceptical lady who questioned the accuracy of his poll was just a minor setback:

'Doctor Gallup, *I* have never been interviewed.'
'Madam, you are just as likely to be struck by lightning as to be picked on by one of our interviewers.'
'But Doctor Gallup, I have been struck by lightning.'

But now that sample polls for better or worse are a feature of everyday life they are more often accepted too uncritically. The sample interviewed may not be truly representative of the population under investigation; the questions, for instance predictions about future behaviour, may not be within their capacity to answer; or the construction of the questionnaire and the wording of the questions themselves may be accidentally or deliberately designed to elicit a false answer. It is this factor, even more than sample design, that makes it possible for market researchers to boast in their cups that they can manipulate a survey (though they would never dream of doing so) to produce any answer the customer requires. It is fortunate that the second of the academic borrowings, from the psychologists, has equipped the researchers with some skill in extracting correct as well as incorrect responses from their victims and in distinguishing between the two. It has also helped in the development of so-called qualitative, as contrasted with quantitative, research, in which the attitudes of a small number of the relevant population are probed in greater depth through extended interviews. When it is affordable, a combination of qualitative and quantitative research is usually more informative than either by itself.

A third academic borrowing source is sociology. For those of a behaviourist persuasion, what people do can be more reliably informative than what they say. Many marketers would agree with this and base their predictions about the future and their commercial initiatives more on observation of people's behaviour than on formal questioning about their intentions. This involves the collection of information from a variety of sources, lumped together under the heading of desk research, combined with intelligent analysis of internal sales data, salesmen's reports and so on. Canvassing the views of experienced individuals within the organization, including those who may be regarded as a bit fuddy-duddy and unappreciative of the miracles of modern marketing, can often be surprisingly helpful – and is too often neglected by over-theoretical marketers.

It may stretch the academic connection too far to relate the market research technique of test marketing to the controlled experiments of the natural scientist. The marketing practice of testing on a small-scale hypotheses about the saleability of a new product or the effectiveness of a new advertising campaign before total and expensive commitment is seldom very scientific; there are too many uncontrollable variables for that, including the behaviour of competitors and distributors and unforeseen changes in the economic climate. A cruder label than 'controlled experiment', such as 'suck it and see', may be more appropriate. Nevertheless, the principle of formulating hypotheses and testing them is a valuable one, giving focus to what might otherwise be diffuse and pointless market studies.

Wasted research

So if market research is based on solider theoretical ground than most branches of marketing, and if most of the research carried out by reputable commercial organizations is technically sound, what fault can be found with it? The main charge, I think, has to be one of too frequent irrelevance and a consequent waste of the sponsoring organization's money. Expenditure on research, in a commercial context, is only justified when its results are seriously considered by decision-taking management and contribute in some measure either to positive action or to reasoned inaction. The response to anxious enquiries about marketing strategy 'We did some research about that, I'm sure it's somewhere in the files' is too often encountered to justify any confidence that this is usually the case.

Five main reasons can be adduced for wasted research. These are: inadequate briefing, egocentric survey design, neglect of available information sources, poor communications between the information gatherers and analysts and the men of action and biased interpretation.

Inadequate briefing

This, though less prevalent than it was twenty years ago, is still responsible for a large number of studies, commonly categorized as 'So what?' research, which disappoint their sponsors' fond (and foolish) expectation that they will produce some startling revelation and so solve his insoluble problem. It invites frustration on both sides to ask a researcher to carry out a study of a loosely defined market, without indicating what kind of a needle is being sought in this particular haystack. Whoever designs the study, whether inside the sponsoring organization or outside, needs to know enough about the organization, its strengths and weaknesses and the market sectors in which it is most competitive to understand what factors are relevant to it and what irrelevant. A situation that offers a vital development opportunity to one organization may be quite without interest to another organization in the same industry with different objectives and capabilities.

The designer of the study also needs to know what alternative courses of action will be considered in the light of the research findings and what circumstances would make one preferable to the others. 'We think that thus-and-so is the case; if this is true we could consider course A, if not course B; investigate and advise' is the kind of brief that stimulates a creative response from the research planner. 'Bring us up to date on the junk food market' invites a routine 'So what?' report.

Egocentric survey design

Such design is a consequence of the specialization that seems to afflict all young professions as they grow up. Now there are not only market research specialists, but specialists in quantitative and in qualitative research, in consumer research, in industrial research, in trade research, in international research, in postal studies, in telephone studies and so on. It is tempting – understandably so in a commercial context – for the specialist to advance his own speciality as the best way of investigating a given question, when this may not be so. So the research planner (a separate beast from the executant) should be a generalist, assembling the information needed to make a marketing decision by the most appropriate and cost-effective research method or combination of methods. Moreover, the planner should not insist on a higher level of statistical precision than is necessary; levels of precision that the research specialist's pride demands are often higher – and more expensive – than the journeyman marketer requires.

Neglect of available information sources

This is a puzzling but still frequent affliction of professional marketers. It is amazing how often outside consultants can go into a strange organization and give its managers important information about their position in the market and relationship with customers, not by any exceptional insight, but simply by asking questions, listening and analysing with the added perspective of relevant published data. It is usually necessary at some point to supplement the facts that are already known internally but never adequately collated and analysed, and the freely available external data, with special market research. But failure to ask 'What do we know already and what more do we really need to know?' before commissioning special studies has wasted a great deal of research money over the years.

Communicating with the men of action

Communication is the greatest problem of the conscientious researcher, who believes that marketing action should be based on a reasoned analysis of the relevant facts rather than hunch; and also believes that his fact-finding and analytical endeavours are wasted if they do not affect the decision-making process. Communication requires a sensible degree of give and take on both sides of the fence that divides the researchers from the users of research. It is unrealistic of the researchers to expect the senior executives whose decisions they need to influence to wade through lengthy reports that may fascinate the professional but infuriate the busy amateur; it is even more unrealistic to expect them to tackle the computer printouts that you still see passed up the line. Research results need to be presented clearly and in context, if possible personally and visually, in order to get the consideration they deserve.

Biased interpretation

Equally the users need to understand enough about research methods and sampling theory to know how seriously to take the results. They may be misleading – the better presented, the more misleading – if the questions asked have not been such that the respondents could give a reliable answer, or if the sample was too small; '60 per cent yes, 40 per cent no' sounds like a substantial majority, until you realize that there were only five respondents to the question, and a single vote transferred from yes to no would reverse the result. 'Research shows' is one of the more misleading phrases in the language; research suggests, but it seldom proves anything for certain in the constantly changing world of marketing.

Start with the problem

Large organizations with large market research budgets will usually allocate a substantial part of the budget to continuous 'tracking' research, keeping in touch with their customers through attitude surveys and with their level of success against competitors through market share analyses. These in theory should give early warning of any incipient problem and provide a yardstick against which the effect of any new initiatives can be measured. If the structure of the continuous research is sufficiently flexible for special analyses to locate the focus of any suspected infection and suggest tentative diagnoses, secondary *ad hoc* research, aided by management experience, should throw more light on the cause and indicated treatment. (The medical analogy is deliberate; the problems of the individual and the corporate body have much in common.)

Smaller organizations often cannot afford continuous research and must make do with *ad hoc* studies. For them, even more than the large companies, it is important to observe the golden rule; start with the problem, actual or anticipated, and with some hypotheses about possible solutions, rather than initiating or subscribing to research in the vague hope that it will turn something up. Following the rule will greatly increase the chance of getting value for your research money.

One small company which used small-scale and relatively unsophisticated research to good economic effect was an international manufacturer of a distinctly unromantic product – steel drums used mainly for containing oil and bulk chemicals. According to its own reckoning it had about one-third of the UK market, spread over quite a small number of mainly very large customers; and it had a problem, or rather two linked problems. One problem was that its eight salesmen were getting an increasingly hostile reception from the customers they called on, who complained of bad service and late deliveries. A second impending problem was that the company was in the process of acquiring a competitive drum manufacturer, also with about one-third of the UK market. There was little doubt that the large customer buyers, not known for their generosity to less powerful suppliers, would use the dual argument of poor service and a threatened monopoly situation as an excuse for reducing the company's orders or demanding a price concession or both.

But was the service all that bad? Interviews by the manufacturer's consultants with the buyers of key customers and with the individuals responsible for calling forward deliveries revealed a not unfamiliar communications gap between the two. The central buyers, in negotiating bulk orders at the keenest possible price, specified what looked like the reasonable delivery terms of seven days from receipt of order; the users, remote from the centre in factories up and down the country were unaware (or at least forgetful) of this condition and demanded delivery only when stocks were visibly low – often only 24 hours before they ran out. Analysis of the manufacturer's internal records (fortunately an efficient computer program recorded date and times of order receipt and delivery) showed that the elapsed time between the two averaged 36 hours.

If they had known the facts, the eight salesmen could have countered the complaints they received about late deliveries and interrupted production schedules by pointing out that far from being half a day late the deliveries were actually five and a half days ahead of schedule. Their lack of information was readily corrected by equipping them with home terminals on which they could get printouts from the central computer of the up-to-date order and delivery position before setting out on each day's customer visits. Detailed records of the overall order and delivery history for each customer, combined with a clearer understanding of the customer's internal organizational procedures, also helped the manufacturer's sales manager when it came to the summit meetings with customers' central buyers. Instead of being forced into hard bargaining about quantities and price, he could steer the discussion to service and argue that the superlative delivery record (much better, according to the research, than that offered by the surviving competitor, but still capable, through informed co-operation, of further improvement) justified the lion's share of the customer's orders at an economic price.

There was a further benefit from the enhanced information system. Having been saved from continual embarrassment by the provision of relevant information, the salesmen undertook as a quid pro quo to improve the reverse flow of information and provide central management with a regularly updated supply of news and views about packaging and distribution trends in customer industries. This was valuable both for forward planning purposes and for improving customer relationships by initiating constructive dialogues about mutual business interests instead of simply pulling the forelock and apologizing.

The value of information systems

Professional researchers may react to this simple anecdote by pooh-poohing the absence of technical virtuosity; the customer research could have been carried out by the veriest amateur. True enough; the whole point is that you do not need to be clever in order to be effective. More pragmatic critics may object that the information about customer attitudes and procedures should have already been available within the manufacturer's sales department; 'Know your customer' is one of the first rules of professional selling. This is much nearer the truth, though the independent researcher can often extract more detailed and more reliable information than the interested supplier; and, fairly or unfairly, his report will usually carry more weight.

What was important was the initial recognition of the problem, the combination of field research with other sources of information (including experienced thinking) to produce an affordable solution, and the effective implementation of that solution. According to the manufacturer's calculations the value of additional sales gained as a result of the exercise, together with sales that might otherwise have been lost, amounted to around 100 times the cost of the research.

Looking into the future, it seems likely that the more far-sighted corporate marketing departments will seek to keep in touch with the customer and the marketplace more through the development of information systems and interpretative skills than through the commissioning of more and yet more special field studies. The marketing manager, worried by a problem or excited by an opportunity, usually needs to make a speedy decision. He will not be happy to wait the several months needed to organize and analyse an *ad hoc* field study, which will give him only some of the information he needs. With a computer terminal on his desk, giving him access to the internal customer accounts system and external data banks, together with stored records of any previous or continuous research that is relevant, he should be able to assemble enough data to construct a balanced picture of the market sector with which he is concerned.

Of course there will be problems, not least the difficulty of foreseeing the questions that may be asked in the future, when writing the various computer programs; the frustration of being told 'We didn't think you would want to know that' must be familiar to all marketers, not least those who worked with clearing banks during the many years when the mainframe computer could tell you almost anything you wanted to know about customers' accounts, but practically nothing about the people behind the accounts.

However, marketing is essentially a game of imperfect information; and imperfect information immediately available is certainly preferable to imperfect information for which you have to wait, perhaps missing the boat as a result. Information systems that are responsive to the marketing or managerial decision-maker, tackling a problem with possible solutions in mind, are infinitely preferable to the prefabricated research study which turns up proclaiming: 'Here I am, make what you can of me.' Information that can be speedily selected by the user from a number of available sources in answer to an identified problem when it arises is the most likely to be relevant and cost-effective.

16 The high-profile persuaders

Within living memory, that is within the memory of senior citizens like me, much was written about Vance Packard's 'hidden persuaders', an insidious gang of undercover operatives dedicated to the cause of persuading the innocent public to buy products or embrace ideas that they would be better without. Now all that is changed. The persuaders, now embodied in large, highly profitable advertising and PR agencies, openly claim responsibility for the making or at least the packaging of presidents and prime ministers, or the successful launch of a vast new share issue; and ambitious young graduates consider going into advertising as the next best thing to becoming something in the City and making a fortune overnight.

Excessive pride or excessive greed, as the Greek tragedians insisted, invites retribution; hubris leads inevitably to hate. The advertising wing of the marketing profession, with its acknowledged skills, should beware of getting too big for its boots and attracting the hostility of the managers responsible for delivering the products or services to fulfil the advertising promises – and incidentally to earn the revenue that pays the agency's bills. The advertising or PR agent is only an agent, not a Svengali, and should have enough humility to accept his place in the order of things.

But urging the Christian and perilously uncommercial virtue of humility is easier than defining exactly what the accepted place should be. It could be said very simply that the agent's task is to present his client and his client's brand in a favourable light to existing customers and to introduce them to new customers. Advertising and PR on this simple basis is an extension of personal selling. The ideal would be for all vendors of products or ideas to emulate the market trader at his stall or the politician on his stump and to do their own selling; but the increasing size of organizations compels recourse first to salesmen or other personal representatives and then to the impersonal tool of advertising.

The trouble with this simplistic definition of advertising is that it omits the factors of image and advocacy. The agent may be, indeed should be, a more skilful advocate than his principal. This entitles him, under the convention of legitimate puffery, to refrain from depicting him warts and all, and to paint a portrait that emphasizes the good points rather than the less attractive. To do otherwise would be to fail in his responsibility to his client and put him at a disadvantage in a competitive environment where emphasizing the positive is an accepted way of life, duly discounted by the public. But a point must come where legitimate puffery slips over the line into positive falsehood. The advertising profession proclaims its belief in 'truth in advertising' and attempts to maintain high standards through self-regulatory bodies like the Advertising Standards Authority. Blatantly misleading advertisements are duly caught and stopped. But conscientious members of the profession remain uneasy about the amount of ingenuity that goes into devising campaigns that convey rather more or rather less than the truth without actually breaking any regulations.

The question of image is more perplexing. Admen, trained from their early years to 'sell the sizzle not the steak', are understandably proud of their skill as image-makers; the 'corporate image' and the 'brand image' are key phrases in the advertiser's jargon. Philosophically it could be argued that creating and selling an image is justifiable, since every individual has his own view of people, products and events, coloured by his own prejudices and preconceptions, which is closer to image than to reality. It is only realistic therefore to expend creative ingenuity (and promotional funds) on inventing images that will improve the relationship between buyer and seller.

Well, sometimes yes, sometimes no. At one extreme it is surely legitimate to invest a brand of perfume with an image of seductiveness that a glass bottle and the expensive liquid inside it do not intrinsically justify; the customer satisfaction lies in the romantic image, not in the sober reality. At the other extreme the extent to which politicians can be sold on the strength of a simplified, glamorized image, masking their complicated and possibly incompetent selves, is a disturbing feature of the adman's democracy.

But between the perfume and the politician there are many gradations where the legitimacy and indeed the effectiveness of image-building is more or less open to question. In fields where competing brands are virtually indistinguishable in formulation, creating an image may well be a condition of success; and a digestive biscuit with added image is just as good for you, if it costs no more, than one without that intangible tang. But it is questionable whether the fashion in the advertising business for ascribing human attributes to motorcars – a 'mistress image', a 'wife image' and so on – and designing advertisements accordingly was as helpful to the prospective purchaser as factual information on performance, reliability and safety. And more recent attempts to apply hasty image-building techniques borrowed from product advertising to large companies locked in takeover battles was clearly undesirable.

Here again the question of relevance arises. As responsible professionals, the practitioners in advertising and the exponents of public relations need to think twice about the context in which they practise their range of skills. It must be a matter of responsible judgement when the near edge of gamesmanship is justified in the client's interest; and when the danger of seriously misleading the customer demands that a line be drawn. This is primarily a matter of ethics, but self-interest also enters into it. If the tone, style and content of the advertising or other promotional activities are not relevant to the seriousness of the subject, it is unlikely in the long run to benefit either the client or the agency. The professional foul brings the whole game into disrepute.

According to *Chambers Dictionary*, 'relevant' means 'bearing upon, or applying to, the matter in hand'. In the advertising context, the matter in hand is the cost-effective promotion of the client's organization, product or idea; and the relevance of advertising depends on conveying the right message to the right audience through the right media in the right language – *and* on being the most suitable vehicle for this purpose.

Being sure that advertising is the most suitable means of communicating with target customers has ultimately to be the responsibility of whoever in the client organization is responsible for approving the advertising and paying the bills. The best agencies can usually be relied on to refuse an advertising budget that is pressed upon them when they consider that it will not achieve its stated objective or that the objective is more likely to be achieved by other means. One agency, for example, won a competition for a government account (much desired for prestige reasons) by declaring in its presentation to the man from the ministry that if it was awarded the advertising account it would not spend the money on advertising. The purpose of the proposed campaign was to create a more favourable public attitude towards civil defence measures against nuclear attack. The agency, having confirmed its own doubts by some small-scale attitude research, argued that public scepticism about the benefits of a select few emerging from nuclear shelters to contemplate a devastated radioactive landscape was too great to be overcome by the most persuasive of advertising. A better use of the available funds, they suggested, would be to equip the local authority civil defence workers with information kits and other explanatory material for use in their neighbourhoods. This would be calculated to serve the dual purpose of reinforcing the depressed morale of these workers, giving them a constructive programme to pursue, and making a start on the lengthy task of reversing the defeatist attitude of the public. The strategy of concentrating a limited fire power on the opinion formers might still not work in a very difficult situation; but it had a better chance of achieving measurable results in what would certainly have to be a long-term programme.

But however conscientious individual advertising agencies may be, it would be unrealistic to suppose that they are not biased, sometimes unconsciously, in favour of their own expertise. If your working life is dedicated to the production of advertising – and your livelihood depends on persuading clients that you produce the very best – it is hard not to overestimate the importance of the advertising solution to marketing problems. So it is essential that the client's senior marketing management should concern itself not with the minutiae of the creative advertising, but with its place in the marketing mix alongside personal selling, PR, 'below-the-line' sales promotion and packaging – or indeed an improvement in the product and product-related service or a reduction in its price. Clients who impose their aesthetic sensibilities on their advertising agents seldom improve the advertising. (But sometimes they have a certain old-world charm. I recall from long ago the knightly owner of a family business observing to the astonished creative director of my agency, 'Ah, yes, her ladyship too has some skill with the pencil', and conveying her ladyship's views on the latest advertisement at considerable length.) But strong clients, prepared to debate the role and purpose of the advertising with the agency, will get better results than those who weakly say that 'You are the experts, we leave it entirely to you.'

Who do you think you're talking to?

Effective communication – conveying the right message to the right audience through the right media in the right language – starts, of course, with an effort of imagination; it takes imagination not simply to define your target audience, but to think as they do, not as you do. Nobody involved in any branch of the communications industry can claim total immunity from the fatal assumption that others share our interests and sense of humour and are as shrewd and witty (or maybe as boring and obsessive) as we are. The first of my many salutary lessons in this was learnt many years ago when my advertising agency was handling a very dull but very remunerative detergent account. We were unutterably bored by the routine of churning out interminable repetitive advertisements, all claiming that our brand washed whiter than white (so different from competitive brands that used other words to claim that they washed, surprise, surprise, whiter than white). As highly educated and articulate males, who had more than once rinsed a drip-dry shirt in a hotel bathroom, we knew we could be more eloquent than that on the subject of washing. 'Have a go, then,' said an indulgent client, 'run your livelier, more convincing ad in a test market.' We did. The new advertising was greatly admired, not only by ourselves but by other agencies and commentators on the advertising scene. And sales in the test market responded – by going down. They continued to decline until the boring old campaign was re-introduced.

The widespread application of market segmentation strategies has made it even more important for communicators to talk the language of those they seek to persuade. Students of financial

service advertising cannot fail to remark on the progress that has been made in this direction over the last decade. Once the advertising of banks, building societies and insurance companies was primarily of the tombstone variety, communicating little information beyond the fact that the organization concerned was in business and had enough assets to stay in business for the foreseeable future. Any financial proposition was couched in language that only an expert financier could understand.

Now the banks particularly talk in their advertising to their various target customer groups in the different languages they consider appropriate to the groups concerned. Corporate customers and serious investors are still addressed in bankerly language, though with greater understanding of their viewpoint in any transaction. Saving, borrowing and other mass market 'products' are advertised in much simpler terms, emphasizing the customer benefits, such as the house or the car that can be acquired with the loan. That this more sensitive approach to communications has been successful is beyond doubt. The success achieved in changing the national ethos from saving for a rainy day to 'Buy now, pay later' may be more questionable. But it would be a mistake to attribute all the blame or the credit to marketing, which can exploit social trends but seldom initiates them.

For the marketing professional the question of the relevant language of communication raises strategic issues. What does it do to the corporate image of a diversified organization if it uses different languages to communicate with different customer segments? A bank which talks fancy to its sophisticated customers and simple to the less sophisticated can give an impression of incoherence; running a corporate campaign, asserting that it is the action bank or the listening bank does not avert the conclusion that it is in fact the chameleon bank, seeking to be all things to all people. On the other hand the attempt of multinational companies to create a monolithic image around the world by running the same advertising campaign in every country usually results only in a loss of communications effectiveness. Consumer habits and attitudes are not the same in every country; the company's or the brand's market status is seldom the same. It is not yet one marketing world.

When it comes to the basics of advertising communications, the medium and the message, the advertising specialists don't as a rule go far wrong, once the right strategy has been agreed. The two are, of course, interactive, with one type of message or creative treatment being carried more effectively and credibly by one medium than another and vice versa. Television commercials for example can be immensely effective at conveying one or two heavy points, plus plenty of atmosphere, but have trouble coping with a complicated story. This interaction casts some doubt on the wisdom of employing separate media and creative agencies, and on the likely performance of the occasional agencies in which the creative and media departments are at daggers drawn.

If the advertising fails it is more likely to be the creative expression of the message than the choice of media that is at fault. There can be primary or secondary failure. It can be considered a primary failure if most of the target audience are either totally unaware of the advertising, when they have had sufficient opportunity to observe it; or are vaguely aware that something has been going on, but have not the faintest idea about the three cardinal points that any effective advertising should convey – what the product or organization can do for them, how it differs from its competitors, and what its name is. Failure in this primary respect can be due to lack of interest in the message itself (the individual eye and brain are very adept at seeing and rejecting the least interesting of the immense variety of objects seen in the course of a day); or it can be due to creative incompetence; or it may be that the creative people were too clever by half. 'Remember that marvellous Joan Collins commercial, now what was the name of the product?' is not a commendation that any agency can be proud of, yet in various guises it is only too frequent a manifestation. The more perceptive clients interviewing a prospective new agency make a habit of asking, after being duly dazzled by the agency's show reel of commercials: 'Now tell me, what was the purpose of the advertising and what were the results?'

It can be called a secondary failure when members of the target audience get the message, but fail to act on it in the desired way – by picking your product off the supermarket shelf, putting their cross against the right name on the ballot sheet, making a major purchase, subscribing to a good cause, or just being reasonable and seeing it your way. There can be many other reasons for failure in this secondary context: the product was not on display in the chosen outlet, it was badly packaged, the price was unacceptable, the cause was not all that good, or there were strong reasons against seeing it your way. At worst the advertising was probably guilty of no more than contributory negligence. However, 'When the product fails to sell, blame the advertising' is a maxim that has given solace to many an unhappy manufacturer; and advertising agents have claimed enough undeserved credit to accept some undeserved blame.

Media maths or flair?

At first blink, buying the right media to convey the chosen message to the chosen audience looks like a straightforward mathematical task, supported by an element of bargaining skill. Syndicated studies of press and magazine readership and of TV viewing will tell the media buyer how many of the selected consumer segments can be expected to read a given publication or have their TV set tuned to a given station at a given time. The agency's computer program will work out from this how much it will cost to buy an opportunity for a target customer to see the client's advertisement in a given medium or combination of media, after allowing for any discounts from the published rates that the buyer has managed to extract. Other research will tell the buyer what proportion of the readers or viewers are likely actually to see a half-minute compared with a fifteen-second commercial or a full-page compared with a half-page press advertisement. He can then assure his client that he has 'delivered' an audience of so many thousands or millions of the right people at a very reasonable cost per thousand head.

The trouble with a basically mathematical approach is that it tends to steer advertisers towards the better researched and therefore more measurable media like the national press and TV (the latter already favoured by the creative people because it is fun to be in showbiz); and because opportunities to see an advertisement are not directly correlated with impact or effectiveness. Intermedia comparisons are difficult; TV notoriously has more impact than the printed word in the sense that the theme of a single, simple commercial is more likely to be remembered and acted on than that of a press or magazine advertisement; but its audience is less specific and it costs a lot more. So maybe the cumulative effect of the press advertising, more frequently repeated and more detailed in its exposition, will be greater.

Also the less familiar media of communication can be overlooked, if the media planning approach is too mathematical. Trade and technical magazines, posters, radio, cinema, leaflets and brochures, direct mail and telephone selling are either more restricted in their coverage, or difficult to measure, or if measurable look costly. But any one of them may be the most relevant medium for a given communications task, or for some part of that task. They may also have the competitive advantage for the individual advertiser of enabling him to differentiate himself from his rivals through approaching his prospective customer by a new route.

Media planning, in short, cannot be thrust into a purely mathematical, computerized mould; and exaggerated specialization down that road is dangerous. Of course it is necessary to define target audiences; and of course the discipline of quantification and costing is important. But there is a vital element of creative flair both in linking the medium to the message and in devising media packages that contain an element of innovation to spice the conventional logic of least cost.

So how far can the innocent advertiser rely on the old saw that it pays to advertise? Only perhaps to the extent that he loses his innocence, involves himself closely in the thought processes of his chosen agency and insists that:

1 There is a clearly defined communications strategy, defining the role of the advertising in the total marketing plan, the target audience, the message to be conveyed to that audience and the action required of them.

2 All the other elements of the marketing mix (product, price, packaging, selling, service and distribution) are as near right as possible.

3 The strategy is adhered to long enough to have its effect (advertisers and their agencies usually get bored and want to change their campaigns just when the target audience is beginning to sit up and take notice).

4 There is provision for regular measurement of results, both primary (penetration of message) and secondary (customer action).

17 The marketing chef

No professional marketer would seriously question that the secret of success is not one marketing factor in isolation, whether product excellence or an attractive price or effective advertising, but their combination in the right marketing mix. But many vainly hanker after a readymix. They long for a formula to determine how the right price should be arrived at, what is the correct proportion of sales revenue to spend on promotion, what share of the pro- motional budget to allocate to media advertising and what to spend below the line, and so on.

A number of successful packaged goods companies do in fact establish more or less rigid rules on these points for the guidance of their brand managers; and it can be argued that the organized mediocrity of marketing thinking that tends to result is the best policy for a large multiproduct company. It can lead to absurdities, like the end of year scramble to dispose of promotional funds no matter how, no matter where in order to satisfy the formula which used to afflict one large American subsidiary when sales had exceeded expectations. But working to rule does often succeed in the individual company – as long as market conditions do not change – because the rules are based on experience of the particular industry; and because doing the obvious thing wholeheartedly and efficiently can often work better than a tentative, experimental approach.

But, apart from being very boring for the actors in the long- running play, this approach will not work when there is not a long history of precedents to follow; and it can be dangerous if the rules become engraved on stone, and do not change when market conditions change. The marketer as short-order cook churning out endless identical hamburgers has his or her place in the tidy and successful organization. But the responsibility for long-term marketing strategy or the solution of an unfamiliar problem or a new venture require a creative marketing cook capable of composing a meal to suit the occasion. Relevance in this case, to add mixed metaphors to the marketing mix, is a matter of horses for courses.

The subordinated product

There was a day – how long ago it seems – when production-oriented companies flourished, and the production manager, if not himself the proprietor, was king in his own demesne. The marketing or sales manager who presumed to poke his nose into the factory was advised to mind his own business – to get out and sell what was well known to be the best of all possible products in the best of all possible worlds. The end of post-war shortages, when selling became difficult and selling at a profit even more difficult, put an end to all that. The accountant with his value analysis techniques and the marketer, armed with evidence of customer requirements, began to ask awkward questions. Was this expensive feature really necessary or could the same level of customer satisfaction be achieved by a less costly substitute? Did a product that most people discarded after two years need to be engineered to last for ten? Was the traditional level of personal service feasible, when machines were becoming steadily cheaper than people? Was it not time for the old design to be abandoned, at whatever cost in written-off plant, and a completely new production process adopted? How about a facelift for the packaging or surface design?

By now the 'product', whether a physical artifact or a service, has ceased to be sacrosanct and become just one component, albeit a very important one, in the total proposition advanced by the organization in its effort to strike a profitable short-term bargain, or build a mutually beneficial long-term relationship with the customer. This could be counted a triumph for marketing in its campaign to shift the balance of organizational power from concern with product excellence, measured perhaps by dangerously subjective standards, to concern with the profitable satisfaction of customer requirements. But there may be just a suspicion that it has gone too far. The more old-fashioned of us still cherish a nostalgic fancy, in our role as consumers, for workmanship and durability in so-called consumer durables.

From a professional viewpoint, however, it is all to the good that marketing, 'the representative of the customer within the organization', has an increasingly influential voice in the formulation of the product or service to be marketed; and that putting more value into the product can be one of the options to consider in composing the marketing mix.

Conventionally it is in the aspects of design and presentation that professional marketing has most to contribute to the product. In one highly regulated packaged goods company, for example, it was laid down that the functional features of packaging required to keep the contents in good condition between the factory and the consumer's home were a responsibility of manufacturing and paid for out of the manufacturing department's budget; whereas the promotional features, designed to catch the customer's eye at point of sale, were a marketing responsibility and budgetary charge. To divide the packaging bill in this logical but arbitrary way sometimes required the judgement of Solomon. It was eased by the fact that the company concerned was one of those that recognized that earning a profit depended on winning the customer's approval; and that everybody's remuneration was geared to the level of profit earned. It was generally accepted that good design could and should be both functionally efficient and visually attractive.

Price as a marketing tool

The belief of the old-fashioned economist that there is a direct relationship between price and volume of sales – the lower the price, the higher the sales – has long been discarded in favour of more sophisticated analyses of the factors affecting sales (and profit) levels. For the practising marketer, price has long been one of the elements in the marketing mix, to be manipulated creatively and sensitively according to the particular market situation. There are some situations, such as a genuinely competitive tender, in which it is essential to be as cheap as you can, without sacrifice of quality. And there is no doubt that, other things being equal, the cheaper product will usually outsell the dearer. But other things seldom are equal. The better advertised product can be expected to sell more than the less advertised or unadvertised. Witness the fact that an advertised national brand will usually outsell the lower-priced retailer's own-label brand alongside it, even though the contents of the two are probably indistinguishable; that the better distributed product will outsell the product with poor distribution; that the product marketed by a company with a good reputation for service, before and after the sale, will probably outsell a cheaper product marketed by a company offering poor service; and so on. Price, in fact, is another important variable to be considered in the market-ing mix, not just the outcome of a mechanical accountancy calculation – adding up all the projected costs, feeding in an acceptable profit margin, and there's your price.

When the marketing manager does have the final word in setting the price (one sign of a truly market-oriented organization) he is unlikely to opt for either the cheapest price that essential costs will permit or the highest price the market will bear. The former is likely to invite a price war, with no weapons to fight with except a progressive attrition of costs and profit margins; the latter, if unjustified by value delivered, is a standing invitation to competitors to offer the same value at an attractive price advantage. The best solution, requiring practical experience and market feel, is normally to pick a price point near the top end of the justifiable range and sustain it by a judicious use of the other ingredients in the product mix, unless and until economies of scale or technological developments make a price reduction feasible. The practical justification for pricing up at the outset rather than down is that it leaves the marketer more scope for composing a balanced customer proposition incorporating such other features as are relevant (including promotion); that psychologically price levels come to be regarded by customers as an indication of value (consultants and other advisers console themselves, as they despatch their large bills, with the thought that the recommendations of a £50 000 report are more likely to be taken seriously and implemented than identical recommendations in a report costing only £5000); and, if you do get the price wrong first time, a price reduction is always easier to introduce than a price increase.

Service with a smile

It is truly odd that at a time when the balance of industrial employment is shifting from manufacturing to service, the actual delivery of this intangible benefit is so often indifferent and not infrequently surly. It seems not to be realized that courteous service is not only good manners but good business. The sales and marketing vice-president of Diebold, which had won some 45 per cent of the very competitive US market for cash dispensers, speaking at a recent conference, attributed his company's success to intensive training of its service engineers, coupled with high standards of performance and customer relations: 'The first thing I do every morning is to look at the overnight service report. We look to solve a service problem within two hours. If it is still outstanding after 24 hours, I telephone the bank president.'

In this country one of the smaller clearing banks, Coutts & Co., retains a very select up-market clientele, prepared to keep higher balances and pay higher than average fees, not by offering 'products' that other banks cannot match, but by insisting that its account managers are better trained and spend more time with their customers and by maintaining impeccably good manners at all levels and on all occasions.

It is a marketing cliché that no sensible car manufacturer will launch a new model or enter a new territory without setting up an efficient servicing and spare parts organization. But getting service or spares for almost any other form of consumer durable seems invariably to be an exhausting and time-consuming battle for the frustrated customer. One can only conclude either that the marketing people concerned do not appreciate the value in customer loyalty and hard cash of efficient and friendly after-sales service; or that they have lost the battle against cost-cutting accountants who can demonstrate the capital cost of holding adequate stocks – and are not concerned with the hidden cost of not doing so. Either way it is a major failure on the marketer's part.

The utilities of time and place

The classical economists got it right when they pointed out that it represented genuine added value for a product to be in the right place at the right time. It it surprising, therefore, that so many marketing managers do not regard delivery as part of the marketing mix. They are content to leave the business of getting the product to the right place at the right time to a transport manager, who may be either floating free at some fairly lowly point in the corporate hierarchy or reporting to the production manager, who in turn is probably more concerned to avoid a cluttered warehouse than to satisfy the customer.

Whether the 'product' at issue is actually a physical product or a service of some kind, the circumstances in which it is transmitted to the customer – what actually happens at the point of sale and on the way there – are as important, in a competitive market, as the composition of the product itself. They affect the value to the ultimate customer and they affect even more the long-term relationship between supplier and customer. Efficiency and reliability in this area can constitute the 'product plus' that marketers are constantly seeking and more than justify the premium price that may be needed to cover their cost.

I am the organization

Another marketing cliché that provokes sage nodding of heads at sales conferences is the statement that the organization's representative, face to face with the customer, speaks for the organization and to all intents and purposes *is* the organization. But how far are all the implications of the statement recognized in practice? Certainly the salesman or the bank manager who achieves a solid customer relationship means more as a rule to that customer than the shadowy organization behind him – however large the corporate advertising and PR budget. But how far is he really an 'ambassador extraordinary and minister plenipotentiary', fully appraised of the organization's policies and strategies and free to negotiate as an intelligent individual, understanding if not necessarily accepting the customer's viewpoint? Is he not more often a harried minion, pursuing sometimes arbitrary sales targets, ill-informed about the mind of his masters and required to refer any but the most trivial decisions up the line? If he is the organization, it cannot be the same organization that the advertising speaks so highly of.

But corporate battle for supremacy between sales manager and marketing manager is most happily resolved when the two become one, bearing the proud title of sales and marketing manager – or better still marketing and sales director. But with or without direct authority over the sales force, the marketing manager who takes a wider view of his professional responsibilities than the mere provision of technical expertise cannot succeed unless he establishes a close working relationship with the organization's representatives in the field. They are capable of contributing more to the extended marketing mix than its impersonal promotional ingredients, and should always be considered as alternatives to them in the total marketing budget. (Is it more economical to find and retain a customer by personal emissary or by media communications or, as is usually the case, by a judicious combination of the two?) And they represent an ingredient whose productivity can be increased at least as much by the application of marketing skills as those included in narrower definitions of the marketing mix.

One way of increasing sales productivity is the provision of sales aids that are genuinely relevant to the salesmen's tasks. The irrelevant and unusable sales aid is only too familiar a feature in organizations where 'Sales is sales and marketing is marketing' and never the twain shall meet. The situation is exacerbated when the production of the sales aids is left to the undirected efforts of the advertising agents on the grounds that 'They are the experts.' So far as format is concerned, whether the item in question is print, audio-visual or some more elaborate confection, perhaps they are. But the fact is that for an agency the production of such material is an unglamorous and relatively unprofitable activity, compared with the production of a TV storyboard, and likely therefore to be assigned to the most junior copywriter. To produce relevant sales aids the marketing executive needs to leave his ivory tower and become personally involved, either selling himself or accompanying salesmen on their rounds. Successful productions will bring the added bonus of building credibility for marketing as a practical, helpful activity, not just head office mumbo-jumbo.

A second way is the route of improved communications. The loneliness of the long distance salesman is notorious. If, through the sales manager, he can be kept in the picture about what is going on in the wider marketplace, outside his immediate customers, how the company is faring and what non-confidential developments are in train, he will be not only a more involved member of the organization but a more interesting contact for the customer. If the information flow is two-way, he can also be a considerable help to the marketing executive in providing early warning of changes in customer attitudes and market conditions.

A third way of increasing sales force productivity is to become actively involved in what should be the unending process of sales training. This may not involve more than contributing marketing modules to existing programmes. But if well done it can reinforce what is already a healthy trend in most well-run sales forces, converting salesmen from guided missiles to thinking and contributing representatives of the organization.

Below the line

In my advertising agency days, as I dimly recall, spending marketing funds 'below the line', on promotions, competitions, point-of-sale display, premiums, exhibitions, conferences, sponsorship and so on, was regarded as tantamount to hitting below the belt. Apart from taking money out of the agency's pocket – a point we were naturally too altruistic to make – advertising we argued was the lifeblood of the brand, the essential fluid that saved it from relapsing into a torpid commodity (or words to that effect). To spend too large a proportion of available funds on premiums and other diversions was to risk transferring people's interests from the product to the premium.

Needless to say, the evidence that successful below-the-line promotions give a quick though usually impermanent shift to the sales of grocery products, that bingo sells newspapers and so on, was too strong to be resisted; advertising agencies, following the principle that if you can't beat 'em you join 'em, set up specialist promotional subsidiaries; and marketing managers took 'below the line' aboard as an important part of the marketing mix. Nevertheless there was something to the original argument, particularly when applied to the extended marketing mix that includes both product and price. There is a danger that the professional satisfaction of devising a successful promotion or the personal satisfaction offered by sponsorship of becoming a patron of sport or the arts, may distract the marketing manager from the more basic ingredients of the customer proposition. As he presents the prizes to the lucky winners, a modern Maecenas bathed in telly lighting, he should ask himself whether the same expenditure on product improvement, advertising or a price concession might have contributed more to the preservation of the brand.

There must be a better way

An essential characteristic of the marketing chef, which rules out unthinking dependence on standard textbook recipes, is creative dissatisfaction. The instinctive objective of the general, production or financial manager is to have everything tidy and under control; the latest crisis is dealt with at last, and finally they can indulge the rare pleasure of relaxing and admiring the smooth-running machine. The role of the marketing manager – not the shortest route to popularity – is to disturb complacency by reminding his colleagues that this is a changing, competitive world and there must be a better way of doing it, whatever it may be. His responsibility, as the main channel of information about the market, customers and competitors, is to contribute more than his share to the management team's worries about the future. Yes, we are ahead now, but others are catching up. Yes, the customers seem happy enough but, if nothing worse, they are bound before too long to get bored with the same old thing. Let's see what we can do to give them an even better deal.

The need to seek constantly for improvements, to ring the changes, applies most forcefully to the marketer's own province of the marketing mix. Changes need to be made carefully and sensitively; people's desire for something new and better is usually complicated by an affection for the familiar. So when keeping one step ahead of changes in relevant technology or customer needs and attitudes or market conditions or competitors' initiatives, it is important to convey the impression that *plus ça change, plus c'est la même chose*. The marketing chef needs constantly to adapt his unique recipes to changing conditions without losing his three-star rating. It is quite a challenge to his creative powers as well as his ability to persuade his colleagues to join in the fun.

18 Family communications

All of you who have observed or experienced the rigours of family life will be familiar with the great communicator, who oozes charm in his office, his personal appearances and his written pronouncements, but is hell to live with. Not a few otherwise successful marketers conform to this pattern, concentrating all their communications skills on comfortably remote and impersonal customers, and neglecting to establish good working relationships with their colleagues and subordinates. It greatly reduces their effectiveness in their primary tasks of creating mutually satisfactory relationships between organization and customer. In all but the totally impersonal industries, like mail order, the people in contact with the customer communicate its personality; and even in an impersonal organization the actions of individuals in positions apparently remote from the customer affect the relationship for better or for worse. So the marketer who wants to send signals to the customer needs to make sure that everybody in the organization is playing the same tune.

Some years ago I did a job for the newly appointed marketing manager of an Irish bank that had previously considered marketing to be one of the luxuries that it could get along without. He was puzzled that despite a steady stream of communications from the new marketing department to the branches, full of instructions, advice and promotional material, very little seemed to have changed at branch level. I asked him how many field trips he had taken around the branches since joining the bank, and he replied indignantly that he had been far too busy to find time for weeks in the country. So I volunteered to take a look on his behalf.

It was an instructive as well as an entertaining trip. I recall particularly a small-town branch in the wilds of west Cork, which the incumbent manager had only recently taken over. His predecessor had been forced to take early retirement due to an indisposition brought on by over-indulgence in the national beverage. I asked the new manager whether he had found the customer records in good order when he took over.

'What records? We don't need to bother with them. We know all our customers and all about them.'

'But you can't have known any of them when you first arrived.'

'Ah, that was no problem, the porter told me who was who and what was what.'

'Well, then,' I said rather desperately, 'could we draw a sample from your signature cards for a customer survey we have in mind to carry out?'

'Signature cards? We don't bother with anything like that. If Seumas's auntie comes in to collect a couple of hundred pounds to pay for a cow, we give her the money. No problem.'

It was an idyllic picture of a pastoral age, when banking was a matter of mutual confidence and bank managers were long-term members of the community, not peripatetic whizzkids. But there was clearly a considerable communications gap between the scene and the textbook exhortations of the young marketing manager at head office.

I recall also more sombre visits to branches in Strabane, Derry and the Falls Road, brought on my own head by a pedantic insistence on visiting a random sample of branches. The manager in the Falls Road, whose windows had been blown in for the umpteenth time the day before, was clearly close to a nervous breakdown. He was operating an open door policy – no lock on his private office – commendable from a marketing viewpoint, but perhaps more to do with a reluctance to inconvenience armed visitors than a desire to welcome customers. He had another unusual arrangement: instead of money in tills, the cash behind the counter was laid out in neat piles on a table – it helped, he said, when the ladies of the neighbourhood rushed in for the weekend shopping money.

I agreed that this was a splendid idea, and rather diffidently asked what became of the marketing circulars from head office. 'Oh them,' he said, 'I still have an excellent filing system; they haven't taken my waste-paper basket yet.' It was difficult not to conclude that in this case, too, the marketing manager was wasting his time and bringing marketing into disrepute through lack of common sense. He would have employed his energies better in joining the great policy debate about the recommended answer to the stark alternative, 'Your money or your life.' (The unbankerly conclusion, I was happy to learn, was that when it came to the crunch, the money – the bank's money – had to go.)

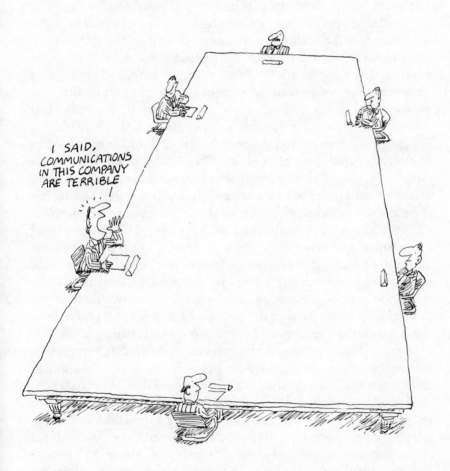

This particular anecdote may seem untypical – well, you know, the Irish. But, in fact, bad communications within the family are typical of almost all organizations, large and small; any consultant will know how easily a reputation for perceptiveness can be won by remarking, within the first week of tackling a new assignment, that 'Communications in this company are terrible.'

It is, of course, essentially the chief executive's fault if the remark is justified – and much to his credit if it is not. But the marketing manager or whoever within the organization carries the responsibility for projecting the organization's personality externally is missing a great chance to win his spurs if he is not very actively involved in doing the same thing internally. The qualities he needs to succeed at the former are equally relevant to the latter. If he possesses the first qualification of an effective marketer – knowing what makes people tick – there is ample scope to apply it to understanding relationships within the corporate family, the personalities of the individuals who dominate it, the individual contributions they are capable of making and the best way of enlisting their interest and support. If he is as skilful as he should be at finding common ground between the company and its customers, creating long-term relationships, he should also be good at the equally arduous task of building a consensus among his colleagues and executives down the line about the business development projects with which he is concerned. If he is expert at information and persuasion, the first place to apply his expertise is within the bosom of the corporate family. It is needed both because of its direct managerial effect on the smooth running of the operation, and because of its knock-on effect on customers; it is a powerful reinforcement of the promotional message if everyone in the organization believes and acts upon the advertised claims.

Finally, if the marketer has all the expertise that is expected of him in matching the medium to the message, the revolution in information technology should give him a field day. Now that every other desk is equipped, or about to be equipped, with a video screen to supplement such old-fashioned communications devices as the telephone and the mail, both public and in-house, there is surely an embarrassment of choice for the marketer who aspires to enhance the two-way flow of business development communications between the centre and the points of customer contact.

The difficulty lies in the communications version of Parkinson's law, that communications traffic expands to fill the routes available to carry it. An organization's communications arteries soon become clogged with administrative instructions, of the utmost importance no doubt to the despatcher, who can feel that once an instruction has gone out he is personally covered if anything goes wrong, and of the utmost tedium to the recipient. It can be just as difficult to make your internal business development communication – in your eyes, at least, of vital importance – stand out from the welter of routine administrative instructions as it is to make your advertisement stand out from its numerous competitors for the customer's attention.

In practice the same principles apply to both situations. A message is more likely to attract attention and precipitate action if there is some benefit in it for the recipient – if not a tangible reward, at least curiosity satisfied or self-esteem enhanced. So it is important to think of the target audience within the company as customers who need to be interested and involved, to be personally motivated to do what you say, rather than troops under command who must obey orders and not talk back. It also makes nonsense of the town-crier type of indiscriminate communication, 'Hear ye, hear ye, whoever you may be', that so often characterizes the large, bureaucratic organization. People react better to messages from individuals they know and respect, which address them in terms that seem personally relevant; so a general message may need to be broken down into different versions to be transmitted through different channels to different groups, depending on their interests and the kind of action they are in a position to take; 'But what do they think *I* can do about it?' is a question that takes the sting out of any action-oriented communication.

Repetition is another principle of external communications that needs to be practised internally. It would be invidious to compare the sublime business of corporate marketing communications with the ridiculous task of training a puppy; but it is certainly true in both cases that you need to say it not once but again, and again and again and again, if you want the message to stick; and it follows from this that you need, at whatever risk of compromising the majesty of marketing, to keep it simple, stupid.

The hierarchy of effective communications media is much the

same internally as externally. There is nothing yet in the miracles of modern technology to beat face-to-face communication, supplemented by other forms of reminder. This is why desk-bound marketers, too introverted to get out and around the organization, so often fail to make their mark; and why those who are concerned with communicating the organization's objectives and personality through its chief executive rejoice when this focal individual is an outgoing character. (There is room for a thesis, if one has not already been written, on the correlation between employee productivity and the proportion of the chief executive's time spent away from his desk.)

In principle, face-to-face communication works best when it is one-to-one and a dialogue rather than a monologue. But organizations soon outgrow the size when the chief executive can find time for regular dialogues with anyone outside the inner circle of key executives; so the dedicated communicator has to fall back on the alternatives of chain messages ('Got the point? Then pass it on to your chaps'), meetings or orations. The chain message tends to get garbled in transmission. The World War I legend of the message that started out as 'Send reinforcements, we are going to advance' and ended as 'Send three-and-fourpence, we are going to a dance' is only comprehensible now to old fogeys, thanks to decimalization and inflation: 'Send 20p' simply would not do. But garblification goes on for ever. Pontification when the chief executive mounts the rostrum and holds forth to the respectful multitude consumes less of his time; but it seldom results in a meeting of minds. Platform intoxication tends to afflict the orator, leading him into exaggerated or over-formal pronouncements; and captive audiences who cannot answer back tend to become disrespectful. Which leaves meetings of all shapes and sizes as probably the best occasions for generating the full understanding and agreement that leads to whole-hearted action.

Meetings of minds

How often have you come out of one of the innumerable meetings that characterize organizational life saying to yourself: 'What was all that about? It must have cost a small fortune in salaries; but it was a nice rest, and now I must get back to work.' Meetings, if not well planned and run, are productive only of doodles; but they can and should be the dynamos of the organization, generating the ideas, the consensus and the energy which lead to co-ordinated action. It all depends on the skill of the meeting's chairman and organizer, both of them roles which the marketer will frequently play; whether he does it well or badly will have much to do with his influence on the organization's fortunes.

The chairman's role of stating the objectives of the meeting, eliciting *thinking* contributions from those present, consistent with their abilities and expertise, summarizing conclusions and agreed action, minimizing waffle, is widely documented. More intricate and more interesting is the role of the organizer, which starts long before the meeting itself and ends long after it is over. The practice attributed to Earl Mountbatten of drafting the minutes of a meeting before calling it, was perhaps exaggerated. But it is certainly true that a good organizer will have a good idea of what he expects to come out of a meeting – without excluding the hope that participants will be stimulated to produce new and better ideas – and will do a great deal of preliminary work to ensure that it reaches a positive conclusion. He will certainly want to circulate briefing documents; and if there are important decisions to be made at the meeting, personal briefings may well be justified. Coming naked to the conference chamber, like some non-executive directors who read the board papers in the car on the way to the meeting and are thus primed to make the earth-shattering recommendation that the accounts receivable figure should be reduced, should not be encouraged.

The individual that the meeting organizer most needs to brief, not to say nobble, is the meeting's chairman (or, if you insist, chairperson). His or her handling of the meeting will be crucial to its outcome. But all is not lost if a weak chairman leaves the meeting confused and inconclusive. The prudent organizer who reserves to himself the drafting of the minutes can perform wonders of clarification, particularly after a muddled meeting, without actually doing violence to his duty to make a true record of what transpired; leaving responsibility for the minutes to a junior secretary can only reduce the practical effectiveness of meetings.

Finally, in the dynamo concept of meetings, there is the organizer's follow-up task, making sure where marketing projects are concerned that the minutes are not simply filed and forgotten and that the good resolutions are turned into accomplished facts.

Voice and vision

Next to personal contact in the internal communications hierarchy is the combination of the spoken and written message, with the added bonus of movement and colour, that audiovisual media offer. The evidence from television advertising that this form of communication is more effective – at a cost – than the written word alone is supplemented by experimental evidence from the growing number of decentralized companies whose branches are equipped with TV screens, either on line to headquarters or with cassette attachments; even home-made videos, describing a new product or a new project, are better understood and better remembered than the most painstakingly written paper on the subject. And if produced in programmed learning, question and answer form, videos can introduce at least some of the individual involvement and dialogue that characterizes the best forms of personal communication.

In some cases also a video can be preferable to the chief executive's personal address to the troops. Well rehearsed and produced in fireside chat style or answering questions, he can come across as a more human personality with a more believable message than addressing the multitudes from on high; it also saves a lot of wear and tear on the company jet.

If a choice has to be made between voice alone and vision (in written form) alone, voice through the medium of the telephone will usually win on effectiveness points, as long as protective secretaries, obstructive switchboard operators and other hazards can be overcome. A personal call from the President has far more influence on a recalcitrant congressman than the most eloquent White House memorandum; and in less august circumstances, you can always talk back.

But I am in danger, as a committed scribbler, of branding my own medium of the written word as obsolescent. As long as reading is not totally dropped from the three Rs of the educational system in favour of computarithmetic, written communication will have its place. It is relatively cheap, so it can be used for repetition and reminder. Its static nature makes it easier to ponder and refer to again. And written messages will penetrate, if gobbledegook is eschewed and enough trouble taken to write simply and clearly. There is no reason to suppose that they will cease to have a place in a total internal communications campaign designed to change an organization's attitude to customers and ensure that everybody speaks with something approaching the same voice.

Accountants into marketers

An industry (it would prefer to be called a profession) that has come to accept the need for more marketing thrust is accountancy. Seen through the eyes of the jealous outsider, accountancy firms seem to have had it too good for too long. The statutory requirement for an annual audit, combined with the belief that it was imprudent to question your auditors' fees or the thoroughness of their work lest they uncover some skeleton in your cupboard, has made in the past for a rather easy and very prosperous life. In some cases the large national firms have grown larger more through a process of mergers than through great dedication to the pursuit of new customers or the development of new customer services.

All that has changed. Customers are unashamed about negotiating audit fees and sometimes – particularly when they have their own internal audit departments – inclined to question the value of the services rendered. Audit fees account for a diminishing (though still very important) share of total revenue, as tax advice, data processing, consultancy, recruitment and other specialist services are developed. And a level of competition long familiar in other industries has brought in its train formal new business presentations, advertising (long forbidden as unworthy of a respectable profession) and other sales promotional activities.

But the people running the firms do not all find it easy to change their attitudes and behaviour. Nor does the traditional partnership organization of accountancy firms help the activists to bring about change; when all partners in theory are equal, even though some are more equal than others, the noes tend to have it; and a notorious appetite for change is not the best recommendation when it comes to electing a new managing partner. Growth through merger also turns out to be no friend of change by consensus; having reluctantly sought shelter in a larger organization for sound economic reasons, the partners in the smaller concerns are in no mood to take the further step of conforming to group strategy.

One large national partnership, which decided that change however distasteful was inevitable, invited consultants to assist in the process. The beginning of what was bound to be a long-term programme of change had clearly to be agreement on objectives. A summit meeting of senior partners was organized by the firm's marketing consultants – whose role was the familiar one of nagging their clients to accept the logic of the marketplace – to agree on objectives and directions. These were to be regularly repeated as the partnership became more of a managed business, with results conscientiously communicated to the rest of the partners.

With a national practice, it made little sense to attempt excessive centralization. While the London office practice was heavily weighted towards multinationals and other large organizations, medium and small clients were much more important elements in the economies of the regional offices; and apparent domination by big brother in London could be calculated to upset loyalties inherited from pre-merger days. So it was agreed that each office should have its own business plan, with a designated partner responsible for marketing, subject to any advice and assistance required from the centre. The first plans were of variable quality – mostly poor – and considerable assistance was needed to make them actionable; but this in itself helped to stimulate the two-way communications flow that was needed – an opportunity for the central marketing unit and the consultants.

Many of the firm's activities, including taxation, consultancy and other specialist services and tailor-made 'products' for clients with specialized requirements like local authorities, did not fit comfortably into a regionalized organizational structure. Most of the specialist services had greater growth potential in a changing market than the traditional services for which demand was at best static. So these were formalized as separate profit centres, managed at the centre and responsible for selling their services both direct to prospective clients and indirectly through the branch offices. Once again there was a need for communications that the consultant-assisted central marketing unit could help to implement and professionalize.

All large consultancy firms have active training programmes, serving the combined purposes of enabling the students to obtain their accountancy qualifications and providing a pool of relatively cheap labour and potential future partners for the host firm. Here was an opportunity for injecting a marketing communications element into the training programme as part of a long-term programme for changing the attitudes towards the nature of the job of those who stayed on to become partners. It was not impossible that evidence of the firm's commitment to change and planned growth would encourage a higher proportion of the élite among them to stay with the firm; even if they departed after qualifying, they would still speak for the firm during their period in training – and, for better or worse, after they left.

It was two years later, *after* the internal communications flow became more systematic, purposeful and professional, and after the organization was structured to turn communications into action, that a serious drive was begun on external communications including advertising (now reluctantly legitimized by the accountants' ruling body).

Nothing very remarkable about this simple tale, you will say. Of course not – except that the consultants were originally called in to advise on advertising, which the partners saw as the quick and easy solution to all their marketing problems. It took a deal of persuasion to convince them that their money would be wasted if they did not first get their own thinking, organization and internal communications in order. It was a question of priorities and timing, not of being clever.

19 The ever-youthful brand

By emphasizing in Chapter 14 the marketer's responsibility for safeguarding the brand and prolonging its life, I exposed a vulnerable flank. Is it not a key responsibility of the professional marketer to be a radical rather than a conservative, to promote innovation and keep pace with change? Is not 'new' traditionally one of the most potent words in advertising? Is not much of marketing literature devoted to new product development techniques and procedures? Yes and yes and yes.

But new product development is also an area with a dismayingly high failure rate. Such statements as 'Sixty new ideas are needed to produce one marketable new product' and 'Eight out of ten new products marketed never earn a profit' are repeated so often that they fail to shock. Marketers claiming the responsibility for new product development are apparently unembarrassed by what is surely a poor advertisement of their professional skills. What's to be done about it?

Widening the concept

The essential dilemma is that an organization which fails to innovate in a changing world will soon perish; but it will perish even sooner if it innovates expensively and unsuccessfully (with the blame, justly or unjustly, pinned on bad marketing). One step which would help both marketing prestige and corporate performance would be to widen the concept of innovation beyond the invention of new products. The pressure for innovation, it need hardly be said, varies greatly between industries. The field of information technology changes so rapidly that only those companies with the resources to finance a large R & D activity and to bring the fruits of its labours to market are likely to survive for long. Food is a different kettle of fish. Actual consumption habits change remarkably slowly; it is in processing, packaging and distribution – the gap between farm and mouth – that most of the innovation takes place. Depending on the industry in which they are involved, marketers can and should consider a number of alternative outlets for their innovative skills to spawning a succession of new products in the hope that some of the products (and they themselves) will survive.

There is the familiar alternative of acquisition. One large UK pharmaceutical company had a policy, well known internally if not widely publicized externally, of seeking out small companies owning a 'sleeper' brand, with a good local reputation, doubling the price, quadrupling the marketing and advertising effort and living happily ever after on the enhanced profits. Things became more difficult as competitors adopted similar policies; the supply of small undervalued companies dried up and the size of acquisition needed to make a significant difference to the predator's business grew larger, ceasing to be one-product companies. On one occasion the company's emissary, visiting the factory of a target toiletry acquisition, noticed a funny smell. 'But didn't you know that we also make glue?' So then the predator, quite unexpectedly, was in the adhesives business. Mergers and acquisitions seldom turn out in practice quite as their proponents predict; the anticipated synergy does not materialize, corporate cultures do not mix, the key people and customers bought as part of the package do not stay bought. But it is an alternative that cannot be ignored; and marketers involved in the preliminary evaluation of prospective acquisitions can increase the probability of a successful outcome by making sure that the essential ingredients of customers and brands – without which no business has a future – are as solid as they seem.

At the opposite extreme there are the modest alternatives of product improvement and range extension. Both of these are, of course, devices for prolonging the life of the brand and extracting the maximum return from it. Much less satisfying to the marketing ego than the creation of a totally new product, they are also much less risky and less costly. Product improvement – incorporating every technological, design or cost saving development as it becomes available, in order to give the customer better value, while maintaining the producer's profit margin – has to be a constant preoccupation. Range extension – using the brand as an umbrella to protect a family of product variations, appealing to different needs or tastes – is more problematical. If all goes well, it should increase total sales of the brand without requiring extra expenditure on promotion. But in the case of a manufactured product it also increases total manufacturing costs, as well as complicating stock control and distribution; and in the case of a service there are also additional costs in administrative infrastructure, staff training and so on. You need to get the sums right.

Colonization – introducing the product, modified if necessary to new customers – can also be an alternative worth looking at. It need not always involve attacking overseas markets. Sometimes new channels of distribution in the domestic market will reach customers previously unaware of the product's existence; many toiletry brands gained a new lease of life when they were first distributed through grocers as well as chemists. Finding new uses for an old product can also have a rejuvenating effect; consider the old brainstorming device of dreaming up new uses for a paper clip, and apply it to the product you love.

Improving the selling and distributive infrastructure, including customer service, is another alternative application of marketing effort and ingenuity that can contribute more to the corporate profit pot than even a successful new product; many customers of many companies might well say that really good service would be the most welcome innovation of all. It is certainly an important part of keeping the brand (whether representing the product, the product range or the organization) looking young and beautiful in the eyes of the customer.

Defining the responsibility

Many organizational devices, none of them unequivocally success-ful, have been tried in the effort to reduce the costly failure rate of new products. Moaning over the R & D department's failure to justify its budget by coming up with a steady succession of marketable new products and giving it quotas to meet is seldom more than an empty gesture; it is not the nature of invention to work to order and it is not the business of inventors to know what is or is not marketable. The initiative should come from the marketing department, whose central responsibility it is to have some feeling, backed by research data, for what the market will accept at what price. But then the question arises of who in the marketing department should have the immediate responsibility for finding new product opportunities, creating the products and bringing them to market. A new product manager sitting alongside the established product group managers? This is a notoriously un-enviable position. The incumbent, inevitably producing present losses in the hope of future profits, has to compete for scarce resources of money and management time with colleagues who are already contributing profits and can promise an immediate return for extra production effort, selling time or promotional funds. Whatever lip service is paid to the importance of innovation and new products, the new product manager will be very lucky to secure the support he needs for hard-pressed departmental managers or to persuade salesmen to spend time and effort on introducing his new product, when they could be earning easier commissions from pushing the old faithfuls.

So is it better to assign the new product responsibility to existing product group managers? This makes sense in relation to product improvement and range extension; the individual who spends his time watching over the health of an established brand, monitoring its acceptability to customers and its competitive standing, is in the best position to judge when it needs the tonic of improvement or is strong enough to breed from. But it does not work so well for major changes and is always vulnerable to the pressure of the day-to-day. Why take time out from dealing with immediate crises or earning immediate profits, for which you will get assured credit, for the sake of a relatively risky future project? If it fails you will certainly get the blame; if it succeeds your successor will probably get the credit.

Then should the political difficulty of successful new product development, and the importance of general involvement, be recognized by setting up a new product committee, with represent-atives from marketing, production, R & D and finance? The trouble with this device is that committees are seldom committed, coming together periodically for a stimulating gossip and then dispersing to resume their regular jobs. So a full-time task force, seconded from other activities and equipped with defined objectives, deadlines and budgets – or even a new ventures division – is more likely to get results. It all depends on people and priorities. The essential people factors are the champion in charge of the project, committed to driving it through whatever the obstacles; and the godfather with a power base at the top of the organization, ensuring that the project retains its priority as long as it has a chance of success – and is quite ruthlessly liquidated if it is clearly going nowhere.

In the end almost any form of organization – or combination of several forms – can be made to work if the people and priority factors are right and if there is a clearly thought out strategy for innovation. The head of marketing, if he is wise, will not lay claim to the whole responsibility for innovation; it seldom succeeds in isolation and it is hazardous to try. Instead he will apply what influence he has to creating the right climate throughout the organization, gaining real acceptance for the much abused cliché that 'The customer is king' and for the IBM claim that '*Everybody* in this company sells.' He will make sure that there is a strategy both for corporate innovation and for individual new products. He will use what influence he can command to ensure that the organiz-ational devices and procedures used to manage innovation are in proportion to the importance of the projects concerned – neither using a sledgehammer to crack a nut nor assigning a boy to do a man's job – and that there is direct access to the appropriate godfather. And needless to say he will orchestrate those phases of the innovatory process in which marketing plays a leading part, so as to maximize productivity and minimize unnecessary waste (some apparent waste is inevitable in a process that must involve a substantial element of trial and error).

Phases of innovation

It would be unrealistic to pretend that innovation is always an orderly and rational process. Major innovatory changes are as often precipitated, in marketing as in other fields of human endeavour, by a fanatic with a cause who will not take no for an answer, by an Archimedes crying *Eureka!* in his bathtub, by a mould blowing through Fleming's laboratory window, by an emergency which puts a pistol to the corporate head. But while allowing for inspiration and accident to play their part, organizations adopting a systematic approach can be expected in the end to outstrip the haphazard.

The phases in an innovatory system which most concern marketing are: strategy; idea creation; validating research; development, testing and screening; and implementation. It is only too easy to go adrift in any of them.

Strategy

The extent of the role that marketing should play in strategic planning is a subject of constant debate in organizations which have a specific planning function. Fanatical advocates of the 'customer is king' theorem will argue that the role should be a dominant one. But this tired old cliché, while a useful reminder for excessively egocentric producers, is only a half-truth. Customers usually can tell you what they don't like but are seldom very constructive, unless heavily prompted, about the innovative products or services they would prefer – and be prepared to pay for. It is marketing's task to create mutually beneficial relationships between producer and customers, in which the former proposes and the latter disposes. So a realistic assessment is needed of both sides of the relationship – what the producer is better placed to offer than his competitors, as well as what the customer is likely to prefer to alternative offerings. Marketing can bring ideas of what the market is looking for to the strategic planning party; and it can take the lead in screening ideas and products for marketability. But the assessment of the organization's competitive strengths and weaknesses and of the technical and financial feasibility of new strategic initiatives should be the responsibility of other departments in the organization.

The most frequent mistake in the strategic planning phase is its total absence, often justified by the simplistic argument that the future is unpredictable, so it is futile to plan ahead. The equally simplistic response to this is that if you don't know where you intend to go, you are unlikely to get there. A more considered response is that despite all the irrefutable evidence of accelerating change and abbreviated product life cycles, the major environmental changes, like the communications revolution, take a long time to get started even though they may accelerate in the later stages; anyone with eyes can see them coming. Also it takes a long time to build a stable organization, with a strong brand image, or to change its character. A consistent strategy over time, with sufficiently flexible tactics to accommodate the unforeseen, is of the greatest importance; and marketing should be its strongest advocate.

Wishful thinking, masquerading as strategic planning, is another source of grievous error. The personal aspirations of individuals at the head of organizations, or the idle belief that the grass in the next field grows much faster without the benefit of fertilizer, take the place of realistic appraisal of market trends, customer needs and competitive strengths and of the fit between apparent market opportunities and the organization's ability to exploit them. As well as being a protagonist of innovation, change and finding a better way of doing it, the marketing man has sometimes to introduce the bucket of cold water: 'It's a lovely idea, but there's no way we can make it work.'

The introverted strategy that is a closely guarded secret between the planners and the top brass is another frequent mistake. Obviously there are some projects that are better kept under wraps; there is no sense in giving a competitor early warning of the projected launch of a new or improved product, or in tipping off the target of a contemplated acquisition before it is time to act. But the broad directions of an organization's strategy should be known and understood by all its employees; it will increase co-operation and the flow of constructive ideas. Marketing in its role as internal communicator can help in this.

Idea creation

The generation and collation of ideas, relevant to the agreed strategy, is a phase in itself, where marketing can play an important contributory and co-ordinating role. The first thing that goes wrong in this phase is that key sources of innovative ideas get neglected. People fall in love with one idea, which becomes embalmed as official policy to be pursued to the death, without looking at what may prove to be better alternatives. Or they become attached to a particular source of ideas, like brainstorming, and rely on it alone. There are innumerable sources of innovative ideas. A consumer need identified by market research is recommended by all the marketing textbooks as the ideal source. But formal research may not be necessary. Customer complaints, playback from the sales force, the occasional customer suggestion, if fielded and analysed, can provide the essential clue. Plagiarization, though not very satisfying to the creative ego, can also be a not unfruitful source. Many large companies have prospered by picking up and improving the product of small companies which have failed through lack of resources; they may or may not scoop up the small company in the process. At the other extreme are the technological sources – developments by the company's own R & D department or by independent research laboratories which open up opportunities in the marketplace. Just sitting and thinking about trends in the social, economical and physical environment can be a particularly prolific source of ideas. These trends are likely to produce these needs among these customer groups; how do we jump in and meet them on arrival?

Thinking, in fact, is one of the more frequently neglected aspects of idea generation. Marketable products or services may start from a single source, but they are more likely to arise from a synthesis of several ideas: a technological development plus a customer need, plus a socio-economic trend – flash – there's a pretty exciting idea. It can be a useful marketing role to maintain a constantly refreshed ideas bank; but it can be twice as useful if the ideas are frequently taken out and shaken, ideally by a multidisciplinary brainstorming group, either to see whether several will combine to produce a concept in line with corporate strategy, or to think through the implications of a seminal idea in order to suck in others needed to make it work.

Validating research

The phase of market research to validate the innovative ideas is the familiar stuff of marketing life, fully described in any number of textbooks. In practice, the most frequent mistake here is for the research to be undertaken before instead of after the assembly of ideas. It is a natural impulse to say, 'Here is a market development that could be important to us; let's do some research to see if it produces any useful ideas.' It will not. Research and researchers can be stimulating when briefed to investigate half a dozen development ideas, which may be true, partly true or wholly untrue; but, however conscientious, they are almost invariably sterile when instructed simply to assemble data without knowing what they are looking for.

It can also on occasion be a mistake to do any formal research at all, in the early stages of validating ideas. The more successful the idea-generating phase has been in amassing alternatives, the less practical it will be to go through the costly and time-consuming procedures of formal research into each of them. A marketer who knows his customers and his marketplace should be able to spot the three-legged runners without going through the formalities of extended trials (though admittedly he may once in a while make a mistake that it will be hard to live down).

Development, testing and screening

The phase of development, testing and screening is where the product or project manager comes into his own as champion, co-ordinating the activities of the various contributory departments so as to give the new product or service the best chance of a smooth launch – and submitting it to a series of review meetings which it may or may not survive before D-day comes. The things which go wrong in this phase, apart from any deficiencies in research techniques or evaluation, are usually failure to observe financial controls, making it unlikely that the project will ever earn a profit; or to meet time targets, making it likely that the project will miss the window of opportunity on which success so often depends. An effective champion can minimize these hazards by exercising tight control and securing as high a priority for his project as it deserves. But he himself may be a hazard, if he becomes too committed to the cause and rescues the project from early termination, concealing the fact that it is not strong enough to stand up to rigorous screening.

Implementation

About the last phase, implementation, little need be said except that feeble implementation is as often the cause of a new product's failure as inadequacy in the conceptual and development stages. The marketing unit responsible up to this stage may by then have handed over to another management group. If so, it is to be hoped that the development team will have involved the implementers in the project and injected a massive dose of enthusiasm before the handover. A sceptical attitude is appropriate in all the early stages of development because of the need for early identification and prompt remedy of defects, or for early euthanasia if the defects prove to be irremediable. But when the time comes for implementation, all doubts and reservations must be cast aside.

Innovation will never be free of risks and apparent waste; that is the nature of the innovatory process, which among other questionable successes produced mankind and all its works. But the risks can be contained and the 'wasted' effort limited, if there is a development strategy which is consistent with the brand that it represents; if the innovatory procedures are well conceived and co-ordinated; and most importantly, if the whole organization is interested and involved in the process.

20 What if?

A vital element in the marketer's job is to speculate about the future, to describe the best of all possible worlds and the worst; and then to initiate action, relevant to the organization for which he is working, that will make the actual outcome (so far as it is concerned) closer to the best than to the worst.

The worst outcome for those who believe in the marketing philosophy is that marketing practitioners should be penned in their small back room, increasingly introverted and subservient to the self-interested money-makers and politicians, and applying their technical expertise in the realms of persuasion to the ultimate destructive end of making the worse appear the better cause. Almost as bad an eventuality would be an exaggerated faith in the infallibility of market research and opinion polls and an insistence by business or political managers on giving people (or appearing to give them) what they say they want without thinking very hard whether it is in the long-term interest of the organization or of the people themselves.

But what if the best should happen and the managers who make the decisions at all levels should themselves become, if not marketing men in the full sense, at least imbued with the marketing philosophy? It might mean that marketing would cease to be regarded as a distinct discipline and be merged into general management, leaving the specialists – researchers, planners, advertising and PR men, merchandising experts – to provide the necessary support services. But that would be a small price to pay for the recognition not that 'The customer is king', which in practice he patently isn't; but that a fair and reasonable partnership between producer and consumer will benefit both partners in the relationship. The producer, who normally takes the initiative in the relationship, will not benefit his customers – to say nothing of his employees and shareholders – by being so neglectful of their needs and interests that nobody buys his goods or services. Equally he will benefit nobody, except his competitors, if he dedicates himself so ardently to giving his customers what they want (which in the end is more and more for less and less) that he goes bust. This applies as much to heads of democratic governments – seeking to satisfy the irreconcilable demands of their franchised customers while keeping the country on an even keel – as it does to heads of large or small businesses.

The marketing role in the equal partnership situation will be, as now, to act as mediator between producer and consumer. The marketing skills of research and communication, supplemented hopefully by an understanding of people and what makes them tick, are clearly appropriate to this role. But it needs to go further than the simple exercise of these professional skills. It is not enough to analyse customer needs and attitudes through public opinion polls and the like, and then to use the techniques of marketing communication to persuade them that what they are offered is what they want – even if it is not. Apart from any question of ethics, you will eventually be found out and the customer relationship together with your precious brand image will be destroyed. Therefore the marketing representatives on the producer side (which is where most of them sit) have an obligation to persuade their colleagues that the reality of what is promised must be delivered. This is bound to be resisted. Changing a smooth-running operation to meet customer demands can be highly inconvenient ('What a great airline this would be, if it weren't for the customers'). So the marketer, in aiming to create equal producer/customer partnerships, has to place the main emphasis on the customer side, appointing himself 'the customer's representative in the organization' and seeking to increase concern for the customer among all his fellow workers.

But in the 'What if?' world of the future, that should be no problem. Managers will take the long view rather than the short view, disregarding the pressures of next quarter's published results and next week's parliamentary question. They will be realistic about the organization's role in the marketplace and their own role in the organization. Producers will be reasonable about the need to have satisfied customers, and customers about the need for producers (at least those who are efficient) to stay in business.

Perhaps yes, perhaps no. But even if you take the view that it is irrational to expect human beings ever to become rational in this way, it is a worthy objective for marketing to pursue. It will mean taking a broader, more strategic view of the marketing role than is customary among today's marketing technicians; and it will require a missionary zeal to infect the bloodstream of the organization with the marketing bug.

Of course this could mean that in time more organizations will be headed by marketing people, or at least people with a long-term marketing outlook, and less by accountants dedicated to maximizing this year's profits; and that the financiers who bankroll them will acquire a similar outlook. If so, it is a prospect that can be accepted with equanimity.

Index